Going Along with Trans, Queer, and Non-Binary Youth

Going Along with Trans, Queer, and Non-Binary Youth

SAM STIEGLER

SUNY PRESS

Published by State University of New York Press, Albany

For information, contact State University of New York Press, Albany, NY
www.sunypress.edu

Library of Congress Cataloging-in-Publication Data

Name: Stiegler, Sam, 1984– author.
Title: Going along with trans, queer, and non-binary youth / Sam Stiegler.
Description: Albany, NY : State University of New York Press, [2024] |
    Includes bibliographical references and index.
Identifiers: LCCN 2023029852 | ISBN 9781438497068 (hardcover : alk. paper) |
    ISBN 9781438497075 (ebook) | ISBN 9781438497051 (pbk. : alk. paper)
Subjects: LCSH: Sexual minority youth—New York State—New York.
Classification: LCC HQ76.27.Y68 S75 2024 | DDC
    306.76083509747—dc23/eng/20231108
LC record available at https://lccn.loc.gov/2023029852

10 9 8 7 6 5 4 3 2 1

In memory of Geneva,
who taught me
how profound it is
to simply listen
when someone tells you who they are

Contents

Acknowledgments   ix

Introduction: Before We Go Along   1

Chapter 1   A Researcher's Escape from New York   31

Chapter 2   Library Time with Brian   35

Chapter 3   La Princess Doesn't Have Time to Have a Bad Day   43

Chapter 4   Scarlet and Popeye Work Up a Sweat   53

Chapter 5   Shopping for Stripper Heels with Anna   59

Chapter 6   Foxxy and the Shoes of Many Colors   69

Chapter 7   Taking the D Train with Yetfounded   79

Chapter 8   Warby's Lost Tapes   89

Chapter 9   Scarlet Wishes She Was a Flat-Chested Lesbian   93

Chapter 10   To Grandmother's House John Goes   101

Chapter 11   Under the Trees at Lincoln Center
with Elliod and Dan   109

Chapter 12 Meeting Axel's Posse   119

Chapter 13 John's Grandmother Has Some Questions   125

Chapter 14 You Breaking Up with Me, Sam?   131

Coda: Landing at LaGuardia   135

Notes   143

Bibliography   153

Index   161

Acknowledgments

The task of writing acknowledgments for a project that has taken the better part of a decade, has seen me living in multiple places, has endured a global pandemic, and has lasted through births, losses, personal heartbreaks, and new beginnings is a daunting one, to say the least. This book has only come to be because of those who I am lucky enough to call my people, and words seem hardly enough to express my gratitude.

I thank the people at SUNY Press for taking on this book. I am grateful for their belief in a project like this one. I am ever indebted to the fabulous Rebecca Colesworthy for her confidence in this work and for championing it through to publication.

Thank you to the staff and youth members of the Hetrick-Martin Institute for inviting me to return as a researcher and providing the space for me to do this study. I've been lucky enough to have been welcomed into the HMI community originally as staff and then welcomed back when I returned as a researcher. I'm endlessly grateful for all the lessons I have learned from the HMI community during my time there.

The research and writing that went into making this book a reality would not have been possible without financial support. This includes funding from the Social Sciences and Humanities Research Council of Canada and the faculties of Education and Graduate and Postdoctoral Studies at the University of British Columbia that made the research trip to New York a possibility in the first place. Funding from the Colgate University Research Council provided necessary assistance toward the efforts to turn this project into a book. In addition, support from the Sydney Social Sciences and Humanities Advanced Research Centre at University of Sydney came at the perfect moment to offer the reset I needed to help take this project across the finish line.

Versions of "Scarlet and Popeye Work Up a Sweat" and "Foxxy and the Shoes of Many Colors" appear in "On Doing Go-along Interviews: Toward Sensuous Analyses of Everyday Experiences," *Qualitative Inquiry* 27, no. 3–4 (2021): 364–73, https://doi.org/10.1177/1077800420918891; and a version of "Under the Trees at Lincoln Center with Elliod and Dan" appears in "Under the Trees in Lincoln Center: Queer and Trans Homeless Youth Coming Together in the City," *Equity and Excellence in Education* 52, no. 4 (2019), https://doi.org/10.1080/10665684.2019.1696253. Thank you to these journals and their editorial boards for their support of my earlier work.

To those who have been my teachers, advisors, and mentors, I thank you for the roles you played in sculpting the scholar, researcher, teacher, activist, and queer person I am today. Thank you to Lisa Loutzenheiser for teaching me what it means to be a scholar and a researcher. Thank you to Ed Brockenbrough for always being the cheerleader I needed and pushing me to be better. Thank you to Dónal O'Donoghue for being the first professor who made me feel smart as a graduate student. Thank you to Susan Woolley for your belief in my work as I made the transition from student to faculty. Thank you to Lillian Rivera for showing me how to lead with humanity. Thank you to Jennifer London for keeping my career going on multiple occasions. Thank you to Sabina Vaught for inspiring me to get a doctorate in the first place. Thank you to Danny McCusker for keeping my body moving. Thanks to Steve Cohen for showing me how to teach with a smile. Thanks to Jeanne Marie Penvenne for showing me how to look for the untold stories.

Lastly, thank you to Lisa Aarli for being the first queer adult to welcome me into the fold when I wandered into a GSA meeting as a high school sophomore. If every LGBTQ youth had a teacher like you, the world would surely be a better place.

Thank you to Adam Greteman for going from being my conference buddy to the bestest of Judys this queer could ask for. Thank you to LJ Slovin for soldiering through this queer academic world with me; I'm so proud of what you (and we) have done and have yet to do. Thank you to Laura Jaffee for standing by my side during our time at Colgate; I couldn't have done it without you and am excited for what lies ahead as we carve out our own paths forward.

The process of writing a book has solidified for me that one's academic colleagues do not necessarily sit in the next cubicle over or have an office down the hall. Rather they are spread out far and wide, leaving meetings largely to take place over email, at a conference hotel bar, or even just on the page. I am most grateful for the generosity and camaraderie of the following people: Lance McCready, Jen Gilbert, Lisa Weems, Brenda Sanya, Sally Bonet, Ashley Taylor, Meg Gardner, Tomás Boatwright, Z Nicolazzo, Durell Callier, Leigh Patel, Elizabeth Meyer, Jessica Fields, Susan Talburt, Lee Wallace, Vic Rawlings, Annamarie Jagose, J. B. Mayo, Susan Nordstrom, and Roland Sintos Coloma.

I thank the students who have come through my classes and the young people I worked alongside earlier in my career. Please know that I've always seen teaching as a two-way street and that you all have taught me as much as I hope to have imparted to you.

I have been thinking a lot lately about the supposed limits of the word *friend* and the place where friendship falls in the hierarchy of personal relationships. The idea that two people are "just friends" seems to say that there could be more between them than a friendship, that a further, more enhanced bond has not developed. It implies that the word "friend" is missing something. I do not see friendship in that way. In naming the following people who I am lucky enough to call my friends, I do so to acknowledge the fullness of such relationships. I am just the luckiest person to have them all in my corner: Cassidy Stein, Adam King, Elle Hauschen, Joe Cristello, Danielle Most, Julia Arazi, Annaleah Logan, Jean-Robert Andre, Israel Garcilazo, Phillip Guttmann, Armen Davoudian, Gabriel Blanco, Xena Becker, Rachael Sullivan, Anne Hales, Glenn Bunger, Derrick Higginbotham, Syd Seifert, Paul Humphrey, Danny Barreto, Raija Harrington Miller, Jack Hind Smith, Angus Shaw, Joel Thom, and the dearly missed Kumiko Umeno.

There are countless others who have offered me pieces of advice, places to crash, shoulders to cry on, sustenance and libations, caring smiles and compliments, and more than a few helping hands—all of which mattered deeply to me as I pushed through these past few years, and none of which I take for granted.

Thank you to my family for their unyielding support and love. Thank you to my mother and my father for always having my back and believing in me, even when I did not. Thank you to my sisters, Jenna and Amy (and Kurt, Chris, Lola, and Leo), for keeping me humble and never letting me doubt that you were proud of your big brother. If I wrote any more about how much you all mean to me, I would have to write a whole other book. I love you all.

Lastly, to the eleven people who entrusted me to go along with them and allowed me to tell the story of what happened as we moved through the world together: thank you, thank you, thank you.

Introduction

Before We Go Along

The June afternoon sun is starting to strengthen overhead as I wait for John on the sidewalk a few houses down from their own. I wipe my brow with the hem of my shirt, as the long walk from the subway through East Flatbush, Brooklyn, already has me sweating. I look at my phone to see whether John had responded to the text telling them about my arrival, but the only notifications on my lock screen are news alerts about the ongoing 2016 presidential primaries. Returning the phone to my pocket without reading the headlines, I take a deep breath to calm my racing mind. John and I are about to embark on a go-along—a type of mobile interview focusing on everyday life routines.[1] I have done nearly fifty go-alongs with John and ten other trans, queer, and non-binary (TQNB) youth throughout New York City over the past months. The soreness in my legs and the long list of questions swirling in my head are the culmination of weeks and weeks of wandering through the city with these young people.

After a few moments, John comes out the front door and walks down the block to meet me. Knowing that John lives with their grandmother who is critical of their queerness and gender fluidity, I thought it best not to be waiting directly in front of the house. We greet each other, and I hand John the small recording device, which they clip to their collar. As the two of us turn to walk down the Brooklyn sidewalk to start the go-along, I do a double take over my shoulder to see whether anyone was watching us. My apprehension stems from the sense that, given the setting, John and I walking in tandem likely stand out as a peculiar sight—I, a cis[2] adult white man, and John who, despite identifying as genderfluid, is often presumed to be a young Black woman.

On John's previous go-along through the same East Flatbush neighborhood, a predominately Black and West Indian area, I was one of the only white people I had seen on our hour-long walk. I imagined it unlikely we could ever be read as peers given that John's size and presentation presumably resulted in others perceiving them as a younger teenager rather than as an adult. It was even possible that other people might read John as a *child*, despite their being eighteen years old. Further, as a gay man in his early thirties who had long worked with young people in educational settings, I was no stranger to the tensions of simultaneously being both a gay man *and* a teacher[3]—that through normative (and homophobic) lenses, gay men are often perceived as a threat to children, thus calling into question our capacity to be teachers of young people. Fears of being read as such spilled into the ways I experienced being a youth researcher, and certainly hovered near the front of my mind as John led me down the sidewalk.

Not five minutes into the go-along, John's phone rings. It's their grandmother. They pick up the call, and I try to deduce from John's half of the conversation what is being said on the other end of the line. It seems that whatever explanation John gave on the way out the door about what they were about to do was deemed insufficient by their grandmother. Grandma wants more information about what John is doing and whom John is with. I sympathize with John as they attempt to explain to their guardian what they are doing, especially since John's frustrated tone seems to signal their belief that they should not have to explain their actions to their grandmother, that John is grown enough to go about their own business. John slowly relents to the line of questions about their whereabouts and starts to explain to their grandmother what they are doing. It dawns on me, after conducting all these go-alongs, that I am about to hear a participant explain, in their own words, what *they* thought they are doing with me. I am about to witness John explaining how they understand the go-alongs, this research project, and their participation in it. I wonder whether John will recall how I had described the research project when I first recruited them to be part of the study. Will John remember to say that I was studying the everyday experiences of young adults? That I had experience working as a teacher? That this study had approval from my university's research ethics review board? That John had signed a consent form to take part in these interviews? That because they were eighteen years old, they didn't need parental permission to consent to participate? That I had told John multiple times that they could withdraw from participating at any time?

I listen with bated breath as John tries to assuage their grandmother by assuring her that I am legitimate by virtue of being associated with a trustworthy LGBTQ youth agency, the Hetrick-Martin Institute (HMI), which is hosting me as a researcher and where John has an internship. John's grandmother might be uneasy with John's queerness, but John mentioned on the last go-along that his grandma's concerns about John attending HMI were slightly alleviated since the internship there was a paid one. Speaking in a more and more frustrated tone, John mentions to Grandma that I am doing "some sort of dissertation for college." While not the vernacular I would have used, John seems to be pointing to the validity of what we are doing together by mentioning its connection to higher education. Because John is due to start college in the fall, I guess they hope this comment will smooth things over. John's responses, however, do not seem to be quelling their grandmother's concern, and she will not let John get off the phone. After a few more rounds of questions, John finally blurts out, "He's basically just following me and seeing what I do each day."

My shoulders tense up at John's description. While it was not technically untrue—I *am* just following John around to see what they did—hearing John say those words (specifically to a parental figure who I know to be unaccepting and unaccommodating of John's queerness and transness) makes me painfully aware that, if described in a particular way, what I am doing with John might be easily misconstrued or mischaracterized. Moreover, given my position as an adult gay man, John's words brought to the forefront of my mind that my relationship to John always has the potential be met with skepticism or even fear, that because our bodies are read as having different races, ages, and genders, my being with John alone in public might always be called into question as odd, or even potentially dangerous. Given my queer identity and the ways I am read as such or not—a reading that hinges on my gender and race and the contexts in which others interpret them—John's stilted attempt to describe our relationship reminds me of the ever-present threat that I just might be read as too gay to be walking around with young people, especially one like John who is read as being young and as not yet an adult. That John, despite their own willingness and consent to participate, was struggling to find an explanation as to what they were doing with me that would suffice for their grandmother, suggests that they, too, are feeling the normative constraints of age, gender, sexuality, and race that shape our ability to move together through public spaces.

As Grandma continues to pepper them with questions, John grows ever more frustrated with having to explain themself. Their answers become increasingly quiet until John's voice is drowned out by the noise from passing cars. Finally, John lowers the phone from their ear, and I look down to see them holding the phone out toward me.

"I guess she wants to make sure you're not a serial killer by talking to her, or something," John says sheepishly before passing me the phone.

≈

I promise to tell you about the conversation that followed when I took the phone from John and how I was able to convince Grandma that I was not, in fact, a serial killer. (If the suspense is too much to handle, however, I return to this moment with John and their grandmother in the chapter "John's Grandmother Has Some Questions.") In starting off this book by describing the first few steps of this go-along with John, however, I specifically lead us to this moment with their grandmother. I do so because I imagine that you, the reader, likely have questions about who I am and why I chose to do this research project with TQNB youth of color. You may well be asking what this "grown-ass man" (as I was once described by Scarlet, another participant you will meet) is doing engaging in a research project that involves going along with these young people as they move through their daily lives. Like John's grandmother, you may already have questions about my qualifications, about how I justified spending time in proximity to the young people, and why I am writing this book in this way.

At its core, this book offers an invitation and a challenge to you. It is both an invitation to go along with the young people and me as I retrace our journeys on these pages and a challenge to rethink how you are making sense of TQNB youth. Through my descriptive and analytical representation of the time I spent with the youth whom you will meet on these pages, you are invited to reconsider the ways in which you envision who these youth are and what their lives are like. As I narrate my own reflexive consideration of what it was like for me in my own body (and the attendant privileges my positionality often affords me) to spend time in public spaces with the youth, I ask that you similarly apply such a lens to the ways in which you are in relationship to both the young people in these pages (through my writing) and to young people whom you encounter in your own lives (even if you are a young person yourself).

In this current moment, there is increasing public scrutiny of the lives and educational experiences of TQNB youth. Trans, non-binary, and gender nonconforming youth, especially, face particularly challenging obstacles in these times because of the recent rise in right-wing fearmongering campaigns. At the time of writing, there are considerable growing threats to the livelihood of trans children and young people (as well as adults) in the form of legislation in numerous states that would make trans students unable to attend school or access gender-affirming health care while also threatening any trans-supportive parents with child abuse for supporting their child's gender identity. Some of these laws are also requiring schools to out queer and trans students to their parents. Moreover, there are growing attempts to eliminate any inclusion of queer and trans topics in school curricula, including the possibility of making it a fireable offense for LGBTQ teachers to come out to their students.

I want to make clear from the start of this book that the root of the problem is that those who espouse those points of view look at youth who identify as trans or queer or non-binary as a *problem*–as doing or being contrary to supposedly universal and "natural" facets of young people. The growing danger that youth face as they continue to be used as a political foil by right-wing Christian and white supremacist ideologies is evidence of a specific (and of course harmful and hateful) way of thinking about TQNB youth and, arguably, the idea of *youth* as a whole.[4] Moreover, it is necessary to see the connection to concurrent campaigns that have falsely claimed that critical race theory is both hatemongering toward white people and supposedly rampant in K–12 schools.[5] At their root, these attacks come out of the belief that queerness, transness, sexuality, sex, gender, race, racism, coloniality, diversity, injustice, and so on are all issues that should not be discussed in proximity to young people. That young people are not fully developed enough to be privy to any knowledge about these supposedly *adult* topics. This is undergirded by the assumptions that conceive of children as being property of adults and that understand the figure of "the child" only through the lenses of whiteness as property.[6] The current attacks on TQNB youth (as well as similar ones that occurred in previous decades) continue to gain traction because of the ease with which certain social actors can stand up in public and claim that children are under attack and, moreover, have their words automatically assumed to represent the majority opinion.[7] The seeming ubiquity of the desire to care for or protect young people makes it easy for those with social, cultural, and political clout to speak up at a school board meeting, on social media, or on a news program and exclaim how children are at risk of corruption, *and* for those claims to gain traction and raise alarm. Thus the central intention of this book is to reexamine the frames through which society is making sense out of the lives, bodies, feelings, thoughts, and actions of TQNB youth. For rather than seeing gender, sexuality, sex, and race as issues that interrupt the normative development of young people, we need to see them as issues that young people are always engaging with and about which they are constantly making their own knowledges.

This book challenges how society thinks about, perceives, and talks about TQNB young people by examining the ways in which knowledge about them is made. This includes rethinking how those of us adults who consider ourselves to be in solidarity with TQNB youth make sense of them as well. Through my telling of stories about time I spent with young people, the goal is to make transparent the mechanisms, theories, habits of thought, and methodologies I utilized to think through and write about what I experienced moving through the city during the go-alongs, including the pitfalls and stumbles in my own theorizing. This book works to blur the boundaries between conceptual and empirical academic writing through the narrativizing of the go-alongs. By writing out and thinking through the parts of the research process that usually get left on the cutting-room floor—the ones that are thought to just be part of the process of getting to the *results*—I shift methodological and theoretical lenses that traditionally delineate and guard the boundaries of qualitative research. The book stops to simmer and luxuriate in the moments that researchers are often taught to bypass or avoid altogether by writing out the research project as the focal event, rather than trying to write around the actions and affects that went into the actual doing of research.

To do so, this book keeps central how I encountered the youth during the go-alongs, how the youth related to me as a researcher, how together we interacted with the people and places that constitute New York City as we moved together through it, and how we were perceived by the city in return. Throughout, the book maintains a critical focus on writing through the processes of world-making that come out of such interactions rather than moving quickly past them to seek out the conclusions and findings to which writing about research is thought to lead.

The book comprises a series of essays about individual go-alongs. In these essays, the writing focuses on the act of doing the go-alongs, including what we talked about, where we went, and what it felt like to be together. Writing about the go-alongs this way is not to say that this book offers straightforward accounts of what happened; they are not meant to be presented as raw data or as simple transcripts of what occurred. Rather, the form of this book eschews the traditional structure of an academic contribution to reconsider how knowledge about TQNB youth is made. It is common practice in academic writing based on qualitative research to present in the first section of one's writing the seemingly untouched data that was collected, and to then, in a following section, offer one's analysis of what that all might mean. To use the vocabulary of qualitative researchers, one's "findings" are often explained in one section in a way that assumes an unbiased presentation of data. For example, a researcher might include a section of an interview transcript or a paragraph describing a moment from participant observations so that the reader, too, can "see" the data before the researcher offers their opinions on it. Such presentations of data are then followed by a discussion section in which said results are analyzed or interpreted—where the researcher works to make a case for what they think the data means. That this is common practice among those who conduct certain forms of empirical research with human beings suggests an orientation to data which assumes that such presentation is a neutral act, that it is possible for a researcher to just show what they saw, witnessed, or heard, plainly and free of their own interpretation. Successful navigation and maintenance of this writing structure are often considered to be hallmarks of an ethical and reflexive researcher. This book explores what emerges when such a separation is undone.

The writing in this book avoids this divorce of the presentation of data and the analysis of it. Instead, the events of the go-along are represented as they are concurrently being analyzed. Writing this way works to challenge the idea that so-called data can ever be presented or represented in a way that remains untouched by the researcher's influence. It stems from the belief that there is no part of the research process that is not already a form of analysis. By bringing the presentation and analysis of data together in these essays, I hope that you, the reader, can better see the choices and decisions I made in doing this research project with young people. I place my theorizing about the time spent with participants in step with the movements we took together and in time with the theorizing the youth offered me about their own lives and how they see the world around them. By narrativizing the theorizing and the analyzing that occurred during the go-alongs (both by me and the young people), I hope that the methods utilized to do this work become clear. By going along with the young people and me in this way, you will see how the time we spent together forced a shift in the ways I think about and with TQNB youth, and I hope that it inspires a shift in your own thinking as well.

This challenge, however, is not just one for researchers. The challenge to norms of qualitative research can be extended to the realm of everyday interactions as well. Anyone reading this, researchers or otherwise, participates in the theater of everyday human interactions. Everyone leverages the previous "research" they have done on other people to make sense of every new person they meet. Everyone utilizes their previously held assumptions and preconceptions about how the shape, size, color, presentation, and affect of a person all coalesce into certain notions of race, gender, class, sexuality, and ability. This book is my attempt to show you how I did that—including the ways I made mistakes while doing so—and to invite and challenge you to see how you do it as well.

In the remainder of this introduction, I explain how I was able to go along with youth (and how I arrived at go-alongs) by tracing my history working in education and youth work settings, and the ways my own positionalities shaped how I came to learn about the young people with whom I have worked throughout my career. Such a tracing will clarify why go-alongs are well suited to exploring the questions I sought to examine specifically with TQNB youth. I offer an account of how go-alongs worked within the context of my project and the challenges and limitations I faced when utilizing them. I explain how doing go-along interviews led me to consider a holistic methodology of going along; the experience of completing the go-alongs led me to consider how the ethos of going along might be instilled into the analysis of this research and the writing that came out of it. Lastly, I close the introduction with some advice on how to read this book. Given my challenges to the traditional form expected of an academic volume, I explain what to look out for so that this text can be read by scholars, teachers, policymakers, and young people alike.

Getting to Go-Alongs, or How I Got to Go Along

To explain how I came to go-alongs, I must go back to my work as a classroom teacher and youth worker prior to entering the academy. Before returning as a researcher, I worked at Hetrick-Martin Institute (HMI) in New York City, an internationally known agency that supports TQNB youth, predominantly youth of color. There I oversaw several programs, including a High School Equivalency diploma program, a college prep program, and after-school tutoring. As I learned what it meant for me to occupy the role of educator and youth worker, specifically with the privileges afforded to me given my relationship to maleness and whiteness, the vast differences between how young people at HMI and I experienced the world became clear—namely, how race, class, and gender identity affected our varying relationships to education, policing, housing, health care, food, economics, and transportation. This contrast was especially noticeable when considering that the areas of the city where the young people lived and spent their time were different from those where I frequented, in terms of both residential geographies and the businesses and establishments we chose to and/or were able to patronize. In other words, outside the time the youth and I spent at HMI, the rest of our days were largely spent in different parts of the city, including in different queer and trans community spaces or, in the case of the West Village and the Christopher Street Pier, by accessing the same queer and trans community spaces in different ways. Moreover, having moved to New York for the job at HMI, I was mostly unfamiliar with the places where the agency's youth members made up the rest of their lives, including many predominantly and historically Black and Latinx neighborhoods in Upper Manhattan, the Bronx, Brooklyn, and Queens.

In getting to know the young people I worked with, I got into the habit of asking them how they made their way through the city—what subway or bus they took to school, how they traveled to HMI after school, or how long it took for them to commute home (or wherever they went) after HMI closed. These conversations helped me get to know parts of the city with which I was unfamiliar. When young people told me they lived in neighborhoods such as Bensonhurst or Ridgewood or Parkchester, for instance, my initial knowledge of those areas was often limited to being able to match a neighborhood with the borough it is in and little else. In asking follow-up questions about how they got to and from those places, I learned which subways went to which neighborhoods and how many transfers it took young people to get there and back. I learned about the young people's knowledge of the city and about the ways that public transit affects how people travel to various parts of the city. Through talking with youth about their movements, I gleaned information on how their race, gender, housing status, and sexuality affected their relationships to space and place, both the neighborhoods where they lived and the queer and trans spaces in the city they frequented. I had stumbled into a habit that not only allowed me insights into how the youth made their way to and from HMI but also highlighted that I knew very little about how they moved through NYC, how they encountered the currents of the city, and how they were encountered in return. These conversations also gave me an understanding of the city's geography that was much more vivid than the flat subway map one stares at while riding the train. My queries helped me learn more about neighborhoods and communities beyond those usually occupied by white NYC transplants like myself.

The research project that inspired this book sought to explore TQNB youths' everyday experience of those journeys I had learned about all those years. Using go-along interviews, the study was designed to focus methodological attention specifically on the moments youth are away from formal educational spaces to explore how they experience moving through the world when they are not near the adults charged with their care or are away from the places where youth are thought to spend most of their time (namely at home, school, or after-school/youth service organizations). As an educator and youth worker, I had only ever spent time with TQNB youth in schools or youth service agencies. As a result, everything I thought I knew about them had come from our interactions and conversations in those spaces. Moreover, when I entered the academy, it became clear that education research about TQNB youth also largely came from work done in these educational spaces. In other words, a great deal of research with these groups of young people was either conducted in schools and youth programs or focused on youths' relationships with teachers, parents, and other adults with normatively sanctioned relationships to young people. This includes the growing body of work on TQNB youth experiencing homelessness,[8] which, though focusing on the experiences of young people as they are on their own in public urban spaces, are often based on studies done in partnership with TQNB youth-serving agencies. This demonstrates that most research with youth, my own included, is done under the advisement of or with the permission of an organization (whether youth agency, school, community group, or family unit). With my research, I sought to explore how young people make their moves when they are on their own.

Going Along with Youth

As a research method, go-alongs allow the researcher to move with youth participants as they go about their preexisting daily routines. Put simply, go-alongs are a type of mobile or walking interview that takes place "in step" with the participants' daily movements.[9] The interviews are meant to occur during activities the participant is already doing. Go-alongs thus make the *everydayness* of the person's life the place of the interview in addition to its subject matter. In this study, the go-alongs focused on spending time with youth outside of formal educational spaces and during the moments when they were away from the watchful eye of those adults charged with their care. Once participants consented to be part of the study, but before we did the first go-along, we sat down for a conversation about their experience with and knowledge of the city. Using a large map of the NYC subway system, I asked the youth to mark up the areas of the city they spent time in, the places they knew, the places they tried to avoid, and how they got around. These conversations helped the youth envision when and where they would invite me to do the go-alongs.

The go-alongs took place throughout four of NYC's boroughs (sorry, Staten Island!). Some go-alongs were vast in geographic scope, starting and ending in different neighborhoods or boroughs as the young people traveled between home, school, work, and socializing—multiple go-alongs included journeys to the end of numerous subway lines in Upper Manhattan, the Bronx, Queens, and Brooklyn. Along the way, I noted the routes that youth took, how they moved around other people we passed, and what their movements indicated about their knowledge of the city. (The following chapters depict these types of go-alongs: "Shopping for Stripper Heels with Anna," "Taking the D Train with Yetfounded," and "To Grandmother's House John Goes.") Other go-alongs involved doing specific activities, such as going to the gym or clothes shopping, thus providing intimate insight into the activities that made up the young people's daily lives and how they made decisions about where and how to spend their time based on their racial, sexual, and gendered positions. These go-alongs provided opportunities to explore how young people made decisions about food, clothing, recreational activities, and finances. (See, for example, "Scarlet and Popeye Work up a Sweat," "Shopping for Stripper Heels with Anna," "Scarlet Wishes She Was a Flat-Chested Lesbian," and "Meeting Axel's Posse.") Other youth, especially those experiencing homelessness, invited me to spend time with them as they passed time in public spaces, such as parks and libraries. During these go-alongs, I was forced to accept that "going along" in these scenarios meant staying completely still and that there were things to learn about youths' mobility in the moments they were not moving. (See "Library Time with Brian," "La

Princess Doesn't Have Time to Have a Bad Day," and "Under the Trees at Lincoln Center with Elliod and Dan.") During the go-alongs, participants wore a small recording device that picked up both our conversations and the cacophony of the city around us, except on the few occasions when I had technical difficulties. (See "Warby's Lost Tapes" about a go-along I failed to record.)

The go-alongs allowed me to move, talk, and spend time with participants as they went about their daily routines—the very ones about which I had always talked with young people earlier in my career. Justin Spinney explains the importance of mobile methods, such as the go-along, in the following way: "It is the hope that by engaging with movement, we will not forget to foreground the emergent and contingent nature of our relationship with space and place; that we will be able to place the senses of touch, smell, kinesthesia on the same footing as the visual and audible; and that we will not over-animate our subjects but instead focus on moments of movement and stillness to understand the ways in which mobile practice (re)produces culture."[10] The go-alongs allowed for a focus on how the young people talked about their lives while moving through the flow of their daily routines or, in some cases, in the moments between their movements. This format accounted for how the specifics of the youths' everyday routines affected the interviews, including what impact my presence might have had on their experiences. Moreover, go-alongs, as a type of mobile method, had to be examined in terms of notions of dis/ability, as movement through space can surely reveal how one is able to navigate through one's daily routines.[11] This included my accounting for the pace at which youth walked, whether they decided to stand or sit while waiting for or riding the train, and how and when they decided to move from a stationary position.

The project utilized go-along interviews to examine notions of these youths' everyday lives and to intimately notice, discuss, and analyze the moments of young people's daily lives that are often imperceptible to and through research lenses. Go-alongs require paying attention to the environs of the interview and the affects created by the movements, including how the researcher's presence influences the journeys of the go-alongs. This is especially true in doing go-alongs with young people who may or may not be read as "adult" and how that affects the ways our ages, races, and genders were read by other people we encountered when the go-alongs took us through public spaces. Such dynamics were central in my execution of these interviews (the moment with John I described earlier being just the first in many examples that follow in these pages) to better understand how young people were making their lives in New York City and how they were coming to make their own knowledges about themselves and the world around them, all while accounting for the impact of my presence on how they moved through the city.

Placing the Go-Alongs

I placed this study in New York City and used HMI for recruitment because I was particularly interested in the journeys that young people took to get to the agency's space and how they made their way through the city after they left. Given that HMI's location in Manhattan's Greenwich Village is far from the neighborhoods where most of the young people who access the agency's programming live, basing the study there would provide ample opportunity for a variety of dynamic go-alongs. While the study was not about HMI itself, the agency permitted me to do participant recruitment in its space in exchange for my volunteering to support program operations. Throughout the study, I volunteered nearly twenty hours per week working the front desk where each youth member checks in upon entering the space and assisting with the nightly dinner service, thus allowing me ample face time with a large swath of the agency's membership. I was grateful to be welcomed back to a place with which I was familiar, though I had to adjust to how I was present in the space as a researcher as compared to how I was as a staff member.[12]

Because roughly fifty to one hundred young people access HMI's programs each day, my being there provided me access to a large group of young people, all of them coming to the agency for a variety of reasons, including ballroom community programming, mental and sexual health services, academic support and job readiness training, housing support services, and arts and culture programs. HMI's members hail from all corners of NYC, some even coming in from surrounding areas outside the city. One key aspect of my selection of HMI as a home for the project was that most of the youth members travel to and from the agency by themselves via public transit, meaning that their modes of movement would lend themselves to the go-along method.

Doing this project in New York City itself was particularly important methodologically. Through my experiences working at HMI, I knew that young people within the age range of my study often moved through the city alone (or at least without adult supervision).[13] Doing go-alongs with young people in places where they were more likely to travel with a guardian might have forced conversations like the ones with John's grandmother to have taken place much earlier and with greater frequency, which would have presented a different dynamic to the study. The mobile freedom that many young people in New York experience allowed the go-alongs to take place without the presence of the adults in these young people's lives. Given that TQNB youth often have difficult relationships with parents and guardians, the spatial organization of and youth mobility practices in NYC offered chances to avoid parental control of the youths' movements. Furthermore, most go-alongs took place in highly trafficked areas that people passed through quickly, enabling the participants and me to blend into the crowd at times. However, whether we stuck out in the crowd or faded into the scenery was impacted by the simultaneous readings of our varying positionalities.

Place is a key element of this study and this book. It is impossible to avoid the presence and impact of New York City both in the narratives about the go-alongs and in my thinking about them. As NYC is arguably one of the most researched places in the world, this book is not the first academic text that is based on research in New York, nor will it be the last. Nevertheless, I work to write about the city in ways that speak to youths' understandings of and about the buildings, infrastructure, people, fauna, currents, affects, and knowledges that all combine to be called "New York City." While uttering the name of the city may strike a chord of recognition among many, it must be acknowledged that such recognition is not necessarily the same. The words *New York* likely prompt any number of mental images and emotional reactions depending on one's knowledge of and experience with all that the city comprises. Thus it is my hope that through reading this book, you become *less* sure of what you know about New York. Along with such an unpacking of New York, I note the importance of place also to emphasize that the theorizing and methodological positioning of this book are not intended to be confined specifically to New York itself. Especially because queer and trans theories have been critiqued for their US and Western centrality, I suggest that researchers can and should apply the go-along framework to different geographic and national contexts in order to experience what it is like to go along with people in different locations.

Those Who Went Along

Throughout the course of the study, I recruited eleven young people to take part in the go-alongs. They all selected their own pseudonyms. The go-alongs provided opportunities for me as a researcher to spend time with participants and get the sense of how their identities and social positionings affected their everyday lived experiences. Of the participants in the study, nine identified as Black or Latinx (one of whom identified as both); one identified their ethnicity as Middle Eastern Jewish; and one identified as white. During the time of the go-alongs, five of the participants lived in a group home or shelter run by one of NYC's agencies serving homeless LGBTQ youth. Five participants lived with a parent or other adult family members, and one lived in a private apartment they rented themself. All the participants had experienced housing insecurity in some capacity at some point in their lives, ranging from those who spent time living on the streets to those who moved between homes of various family members at some time in their past. Four of them were enrolled in the City University of New York (CUNY) system, a collection of public two- and four-year postsecondary institutions. Two were finishing high school, and one was in a High School Equivalency exam prep program. Some of the participants had paid internships through HMI programming; others had jobs elsewhere, mainly working as child-care providers and in retail positions.

Explaining how go-alongs assist researchers in considering how their own positionality affects how they interpret that of their participants, Nicholas A. Scott writes that through this type of interview, "researchers and participants can more readily explore and deeply reflect upon the [participant's] stream of perceptions, memories and experiences and how these relate to, and flow from, specific social and material contexts."[14] Go-alongs help researchers move beyond simple notions of identity and see how participants are read and perceived by others and how said reading affects their movements through the city. This is especially true considering the ways that participants' racial and gender identities along with their housing status impact their ability to access and move through public spaces. (See, for example, "Library Time with Brian," "La Princess Doesn't Have Time to Have a Bad Day," "Foxxy and the Shoes of Many Colors," or "Under the Trees at Lincoln Center with Elliod and Dan.")

Age also played a significant factor. While the study was originally intended to focus on youth ages fifteen to twenty-five, all eleven participants were between eighteen and twenty-two years old during the go-alongs. Nonetheless, I use the term *youth* throughout this book in a way that encompasses the temporal and developmental fuzziness that all participants were experiencing—namely, the shedding of the remaining vestiges of childhood while still feeling unsure about their foothold into adulthood.[15] Whether John would be read as a *child*, a *teen*, or a *young adult* while we moved down the sidewalk together is just one example of how participants and I were perceived differently based on where we were and who was around us. During the go-alongs, I was in my early thirties and recognized that I was (likely) in the oldest age range where I might be accidentally read as "youth." On the other hand, since all my participants hovered around twenty years old, they were at an age when it was often beneficial for them to lean into looking older when possible. They knew it was often advantageous for them to be read not as a child or teen but as an adult. The privileges of my racialization and gender presentation also played a factor in how I was perceived alongside participants. As a man of European and Jewish heritage who is read as white, I can move through public spaces with certain privileges, namely being less likely to be stopped by police in public spaces. Numerous participants expressed that my being with them as they rode the subway or moved through the city stood to make their journeys safer, explaining that my body would deflect some of the unwanted attention they get from people they encounter in their daily lives. (See "Foxxy and the Shoes of Many Colors" and "Scarlet Wishes She Was a Flat-Chested Lesbian.") In other moments, my positionality thrust itself into the plots of the go-alongs in ways with which the young people and I, individually and collectively, had to grapple. (See "Scarlet and Popeye Work Up a Sweat," "Shopping for Stripper Heels with Anna," and "You Breaking Up with Me, Sam?")

In terms of my own positionality, I note here that I alternate between describing the pieces of my identity as fact and pointing to the ways that such categories are always the result of the ways in which my body is read. I recognize this tension because I believe it speaks to the complexities inherent to categories and identities. While acknowledging that I experience a great deal of social privilege due to the ways I am read as and assumed to be white, male, and cisgender, I nevertheless am not interested in claiming any of those terms as identities. To do so would further strengthen said categories as immutable and natural, rather than

as the result of specific ways of knowing and understanding political identities. This thinking is shaped by much of the literature cited throughout,
namely work by feminist scholars of color and queer and trans theorists
who, in their own ways, call for critical approaches to conceiving of the
terms we use to describe ourselves. In particular, one piece of advice from
education scholar Dr. Gloria Ladson-Billings stands out in this regard.
Once, during a question-and-answer session after a keynote address, I
heard her field a question from a white teacher who asked how they could
best support their students of color. Ladson-Billings, who is responsible
for introducing critical race theory to the field of education,[16] replied
simply: *You don't have to participate in being white.* What I took from this,
and how it applies to how I represent myself (and the young people) in
this book, is that to claim "white" as identity does not rectify the social
and political inequities caused by normative understandings of race and
racism, but rather only serves to reify racial categories as set in stone
and universal. I heed similar advice from Finn Enke's theorizing about
cisgender as a category meant to imply "not trans" and the ways that such
an understanding, despite how it is used to imply allyship to trans people
and communities, does more to undergird transphobic logics than undo
them.[17] That being said, I hope that while reading about my experiences
with the young people, you see references to my identities, body, and
racial and gendered presentations as always in the process of being formed
and unformed. Even when I take the more simplistic narrative route and
write about them seemingly as fact, I mean for you to always keep them
under the microscope.

The multitude of possible reactions to my being together with participants, however, stayed at the forefront of my mind during the go-alongs.
It was certainly on my mind while going along with John near their
grandmother's house in a predominantly Black neighborhood where my
whiteness might draw attention or even suspicion, especially as I moved
in tandem with John. (See both "To Grandmother's House John Goes"
and "John's Grandmother Has Some Questions.") Readings of my body
were certainly on my mind during a go-along with Anna, a Black woman
in her early twenties, when she took me to an adult novelty store in the
Bronx. She wanted to buy new outfits, as she had just started working
as an exotic dancer. As the salesclerk, who was also a Black woman,
answered Anna's questions about stilettos and lingerie, I wondered what
she thought I was doing there with Anna. Did she think I was Anna's gay
friend there to provide fashion advice? Maybe she assumed I was Anna's

john? Despite the questions running through my head, the clerk seemed more concerned about making a sale with Anna than paying any attention to me. This was a helpful reminder that sometimes the researcher might just blend into the scenery, if only for a moment. (This go-along is further described in "Shopping for Stripper Heels with Anna.")

There were also times when it became clear that the participants were concerned that my being with them might have certain implications they had not previously considered before embarking on a go-along, especially given the mobile nature of the method. These concerns arose in the moments when the go-alongs moved us over certain geographic boundaries when youth realized that while they were okay being with me where we started the interview, they were less comfortable with my presence in the location where we ended up. On another go-along with Anna, we visited two grocery stores near the 72nd Street subway station on the Upper West Side. When she bought far more food than she could carry herself, I offered to help carry the haul on her ride home; at the time, she was staying with her aunt almost eighty blocks further uptown in Harlem. When we arrived at the apartment building, she expressed apprehension about my coming into the building because she did not want to explain to her aunt what she was doing with me. However, she could not carry all the bags of food herself. We decided on having me come up to drop the bags at the apartment door and then leave before she unlocked the door and went inside. Whether intentionally or not, Anna may well have used the go-along to her advantage to buy more food than her usual grocery runs allowed, thus saving her an extra trip. Along the way, she realized that her choice resulted in allowing me into parts of her life she was not sure she wanted me to see and/or where my proximity to her might be called into question.

Beyond official identity categories and social positions, there was one commonality that most of the participants shared: they were young people who spent a great deal of time by themselves and who largely made their moves through the city alone. Contrary to assumptions about young people always moving together in large groups, nearly all the participants I worked with traveled through the city and spent a significant part of their day by themselves—the exception being Dan and Elliod, who always moved as a pair. (See "Under the Trees at Lincoln Center with Elliod and Dan.") Although the participants were not without friends or support systems, that they were often alone while moving through the city (and during their time at HMI) played a role in their agreeing to take part in the go-alongs. I believe there are two reasons for this, one having to do with my recruitment methods and one to do with the nature of the go-along itself.

When recruiting in HMI's space, I had serious conversations with dozens of young people about joining the study, though only the eleven agreed to take part.[18] Having these conversations during the agency's programs, I found it easier to strike up conversations with young people who spent time alone as opposed to those who moved around the space with groups of friends. This is important to note, as it both reveals the limits of my own recruitment strategies and shines light on aspects of the go-along as a method. My recruitment practices aside, given the intimate nature of the go-alongs, I believe it was difficult for some young people to imagine doing them if their daily routines involved traveling through the city with one or more peers by their side. While there were certainly many reasons youth declined to participate, this was certainly a significant one.

Nearly all the participants who did take part in the study typically arrived at and left HMI solo. This not only suggests that the go-along method might have worked better given participants' habit of solitary movements but also highlights that taking part in the go-alongs might have been advantageous for them. During a preliminary conversation with Foxxy as they were about to sign the participant consent form, I explained to them how I had designed the study to minimize potential risk for the participants. Foxxy stopped me mid-sentence and asked, "What do you mean risk?" They went on to explain with no uncertainty that my moving along with Foxxy would make their commutes safer, implying that my body might act as a buffer to the daily transphobic slights Foxxy receives as a genderqueer person. In the essays, I draw particular attention to moments when the youth seemed to use their proximity to my body and positionality to their advantage, thus challenging norms related to the researcher–participant relationship. (See, for instance, "La Princess Doesn't Have Time to Have a Bad Day," "Scarlet and Popeye Work Up a Sweat," and "Foxxy and the Shoes of Many Colors.")

After the Go-Alongs

After completing the fieldwork stage of my research, I sat with the memories and remnants of the go-alongs for months and months. I listened and relistened to the recordings of the interviews. Hearing the young people in conversation with me amid the background noises of the city, I was transported back to the sidewalks, park benches, subway cars, and shops where the go-alongs took place and was moved and intrigued and perplexed anew about what the young people had shared with me—about the parts of their lives they had offered to this study. I wrote as I listened, trying to connect things that were captured on the tapes to what I remembered feeling, seeing, and thinking. I wrote about that which had been stuck in my mind since the moment they happened, and I wrote about the things that happened during the go-along that I only remembered after listening to the tapes many months later. I read through my fieldnotes and compiled the writings I had done before, between, and after the go-alongs. The more I wrote about them, the more I struggled to find a way to compose anything cohesive that seemed to "fit" the experience. I was initially left dumbfounded by the pressure of trying to convert the wonderfully complex experiences of doing the go-along into "data." All the normative processes of sorting, coding, compiling, and analyzing felt disingenuous—as though they would not honor what the young people shared with me and what we had experienced together.

The trained researcher in me knew that the next logical steps were to transcribe and analyze and synthesize and write. There were well-defined paths that told me what to do with all this "data." This was supposed to be the phase during which I wove the nearly fifty go-alongs together to find themes and demonstrate how, through connections to theory, I was creating links among these go-alongs and making sense of them. However, I could not bring myself to do any of that. None of it felt like the proper way to treat what the youth had offered during the go-alongs. I struggled to splice the go-alongs together, to try to draw out conclusions based on similarities that I might have gleaned between various participants during different go-alongs. Each of the go-alongs felt so different, so specific, and so rooted in the individual experiences of each young person. I wanted to find a way to communicate what the youth had shared with me, the moments that had transpired between us, so that whoever might read what I wrote would be able to go along with us.

Although designed to focus on everyday moments, on the seemingly less perceptible parts of young people's daily lives, each go-along seemed to unfold into a sweeping saga of urban movement, of taking refuge among the currents of the city, and of trying to speak over, through, or with the noises of New York City. Each go-along was an event unto itself, each deserving of its own narrative detail and its own accounting of what transpired between the young person, the city, and me. In turning to existing literature about go-alongs for assistance, I found I was not alone in my desire for different approaches to analyzing the data produced from go-alongs. During my initial attempts at data analysis, I reached out to Margarethe Kusenbach, who first developed the method, for advice on how to more creatively analyze the go-alongs. She shared that I had likely stumbled upon a hole in the literature at the time.[19] In the time since our correspondence, I have been among a group of scholars who are thinking in innovative ways about how to represent what transpires during go-along interviews.[20] As Phillip Vannini and April Vannini explain about walk-alongs (a type of go-along), "Methodological literature on walk-alongs and a great deal of the actual research conducted through walk-alongs still suffer from many of the same ailments that go-along methods were devised to cure. Walk-alongs, by and large, are still too often informed by textualism, cognitivism, and representationalism. Walk-alongs are too often not sensuous enough, not spatialized enough, not mediated coherently enough, and not imaginative enough."[21] I worked toward a style of writing that accounted for the sensuous aspects of the go-alongs, the feelings and affects that rippled through the go-alongs but might not have been discussed or captured on the recording. I wanted to find a way to offer vivid images of the places where the go-alongs happened and the ways those places impacted the movement and flow of the interviews—or, perhaps, a differently vivid image than the one that is expected. This shift in writing enabled me to reflect on the structure of the research process itself, at least how it is normatively expected to occur. I could show the go-alongs as relational and reflective of the relationships that developed between the participants and me through the act of my being in their company.

What emerged from this process was a form of writing that focused on going along as a methodology, not just a method. This way of writing focused more on telling the story of how the go-alongs happened than trying after the fact to explain and determine what happened during the go-alongs. In short, it offered a different way to consider moving, thinking, and being with young people. The specific story of each go-along became important to tell as a narrative of the time spent, the topics covered, and the relationships that developed along the way. The way to present, most ethically and respectfully, what occurred during the go-alongs was to narrate them as stand-alone events, as stories of the moments we shared together and the time the participants allowed me to be with them. The essays that make up this book follow the movements traveled and the conversations that transpired with participants during the go-alongs. Each essay follows the course of a particular go-along to provide an account of the experiences of my moving and being together with the participants throughout New York City. They highlight not just what was said during our time together but the evolution of the dialogue given the circumstances of the relationships between the participants and me, the places where we were located or through which we were passing, and our interactions with the ebbs and flows of the city. Along the way, I draw connections between the theories that the young people developed about themselves and their understandings of their place with society to scholarly theories about youth and growing up, gender and sexuality, race, urban environments, and research methodologies. By being composed in a narrative manner, the essays compel readers to examine how the youth come to be seen through the writing. This narrative maneuver offers new paths into writing and reading academic research. It is one that asks that the theorizing by young people add necessary complexity and texture to theories about them that are published by academic publishers, utilized by education professionals, or espoused by the public.

Writing Along, or toward a Methodology of Going Along

The essays in this book explore an innovative form of writing qualitative interview-based research, one that builds on the idea of going along as a methodology. The form itself is a narrative style of writing that gives an account of the actions of the research itself and tells the story of what happened during the go-alongs themselves. It might be argued that such stories have limits, that narratives can only be read in one way. This book, however, posits that stories have the potential to open, rather than fore-close. Such a stance echoes the advice of Kathleen Stewart, who argues, "Rather than complete or 'exemplify' a thought, narratives produce a further searching."[22] This form of writing positions narratives about research that work against the terminal assumptions about storytelling. It maintains that any one research product is always limited, always incomplete, and always contextual to the moments and spaces where it was produced. As such, the form of writing about research explored in this book does not and should not lead you to a firm and holistic knowledge about the people described in the writing. Rather, it offers you one perspective into understanding their lives, along with an invitation to continue to think with them as you go along your own life after you have finished reading.

Traditionally, interview-based research focuses critical attention on what is said during interviews; it is often assumed that the data is limited to the finite number of things that were spoken out loud. However, this form's attention on describing the actions of the researcher and participant(s) works to elucidate the methodological decisions, assumptions, and processes that are often ignored in the writing of and about a research study. Such attention, rather than focusing solely on the things participants say, makes the doing of research the primary analytical target. This form of writing narrativizes while concurrently analyzing such aspects as the relationship between researcher and participant, how the setting and location of the interview affect the conversation, reflections on the researcher's methodological choices during the interview, and affective dimensions of the interview that are neither spoken nor audible to any recording device. This refocusing of attention to these aspects proliferates the amount of data that is open to be analyzed and considered.

The writing of this book shifts the inquiry away from a sole focus on participants to include an examination of the study itself. The narrative essays are written toward the goal of homing in on the act of coming to know about the participants through the go-alongs rather than, necessarily, what preexisting facts are to be known about them. It shifts the ethnographic gaze away from the people in this study and onto the flows and streams of knowledge that lead toward what is thought to be known. Here, I pull on Ernesto Javier Martínez's theorizing on how stories about queer and trans race narratives become intelligible to the social world. He advocates "for more familiarity with these knowledges and subjectivities, not on the grounds that they explain everything about the social world, or that they explain the social world well in every instance, but on the grounds they are attempts at epistemic decolonization, and that as such, they represent possibilities for new knowledge and social critique."[23] The writing of the book demonstrates how I worked to listen for and hear such knowledges and subjectivities, especially in the moments when they forced a reconsideration of my own epistemologies.

This form of writing takes up a challenge to writers and readers, one that draws on a question asked by Kathleen Stewart: "What if, instead, we build concepts that make it possible to venture out into the life from which they emerge? Concepts that are crystallizations filled with the potentiality of dissolution."[24] This book is an experiment in writing qualitative research in a form that eschews the traditional formatting in which research is often expected to be organized. This book focuses on analyzing, theorizing, and representing the moments of doing the research—the way participants answered my questions, my reactions to their comments, the ways our relationships developed, how we encountered other people as the interviews transpired, and so on. What you read is a collection of my memories about the interviews, substantiated by the recordings of the interviews, the notes I have from the field, and the writing I have done in the years since.

The essays are written in the present tense to give the effect that the stories are unfolding in front of your eyes. You are invited to *go along* with the action of the interviews. How you see the stories unfold will of course depend on how you see what I have written about what transpired. You may think that you would have asked a different follow-up question or followed a different analytical thread in the writing. In fact, I hope you do. I am presenting just one way of thinking about the events that took place during the go-alongs. There is no way for me to write the whole story and no way for you (nor I) to fully get to know the young people described in these pages. Nonetheless, writing out narratives of the interviews themselves is an ethical positioning that reiterates Petra Hendry's question to researchers: "How might we conceptualize our relationship to narrative in ways that don't reify a view of narrative as explanatory or as representational?"[25] This form of narrative writing ensures that I, as the researcher, keep my analysis of these young people to the moments they gave to the study. It respects that *participant* is only ever a temporary label, that the young people who participated in this study and who are described in the following pages ceased to be participants when fieldwork for this study ended years ago. These essays do not try to lead you toward one fixed point but ask that you see where they take you.

The writing of these essays places analysis of the research in step with the action of the interviews themselves. This process works against the idea that, as Elizabeth Ellsworth explains, "Knowledge, once it is defined, taught, and used as a 'thing made' is dead."[26] Instead, these essays work to dismantle knowledge as it is being made. They blend the two processes of doing research and analyzing it by narrativizing my analyses of the moments of the interviews throughout the description of the events that took place. The analyses themselves are layered; they convey an amalgamation of years of thinking, despite being narrated into one story. Some of the analyses are thoughts that germinated during the interviews or shortly after, and others are ones I have had in the many writings and rewritings of these essays in the years since the go-alongs took place. The *me* represented in pages is depicted as having many thoughts that did not, in fact, all occur during the go-alongs themselves. But in giving the former me the benefit of years of thinking and reflecting about this study, I embrace queer senses of temporality into my writing, as José Esteban Muñoz explains, by looking "beyond a narrow version of the here and now on which so many around us who are bent on the normative count."[27] The analyses are imbued with ideas gathered from my moving forward and backward in time. As you read the essays, I invite you to take the time to see what has been gathered and the methods used to do so as you come to learn about the youth described in this book.

The writing in the pages ahead leads you through atypical patterns of presenting and representing research. You will, in a sense, go along with the stories in the pages that follow. I suggest that doing so will compel you as a reader to examine how you are encountering the youth and the study, as well as how we all encounter systems of knowledge that, while socially constructed, are often experienced as being completely and utterly immovable. The form of writing offered here is what I see as the best reflection of the time I spent with the young people who took part in this research project.

Going Along with This Book

This book is meant to represent a coming to terms with complexities inherent in the process of embodying the position of researcher; it is about what it was like to do research with the participants in this study. I seek to show you not *what their lives are like* but rather *what it was like for me to witness their lives*. I want to dissuade you from seeing any word of these essays as some sort of naturalistic observation; they are unequivocally analytical products of my presence alongside the participants and of how their presence impacted the scope of the study. The writing of this book keeps the focus on the experiences of witnessing and making sense of the lives of other people by narrativizing the moments that caused me to think harder, differently, patiently, and compassionately. The moments where I questioned myself, my body, my thinking, my methods, and my presence in the participants' lives.

In starting this volume about queer and trans young adults with an explanation of myself, the researcher, I recognize the risk of making my body too central in the telling of the stories of participants' lives. I am also keenly aware that as a queer person who is read as white and cis writing about a study with queer and trans youth of color, I might be perceived as replicating the long histories of many, many white men who have problematically written about other people. Let me be the first to admit that I am moving through troubled territory here. However, I am attempting to maneuver this space considering Eve Tuck and K. Wayne Yang's advice on how researchers can work against settler colonial knowledge being foundational to the practice and process of qualitative research. They explain: "Analytic practices of refusal can help researchers and the people who prepare researchers to avoid building our/their careers upon the pain of others."[28] While describing the moments I spent with participants, the writing shifts the analytical lens away from the youth and onto the ways I positioned my body and my thinking in relation to them. The writing is composed in a way to continually remind you that what you are reading is the result of a research project and not just a description of the participants' lives that magically ended up on the page.

In beginning with a discussion of myself as a researcher, I position this book as a reflection on the process of doing research with other people and, to be quite clear, on what a strange endeavor it is to do so. Again, I *was* just following John around trying to see what they did each day; John wasn't wrong to describe the study as such to their grandmother. Nonetheless, I seek to avoid allowing this book to fall into the all too frequent trap of having the researcher's voice be obfuscated through a disembodied, unattached "I" speaking from a supposedly unquestionable authoritative position about the lives of young people.[29] I do not want you to walk away from this book thinking you have gathered some unbiased reflection on the lives of the young people with whom I worked. By intentionally writing myself into the narrative of the research study, I show how my body was always in relation with—standing or sitting or moving beside—the bodies of the participants. I was there asking questions about their everyday experiences as they talked about their daily routines, their hopes and dreams, and the things in life that perplexed them. The microphone I bought was clipped to their lapels, catching their responses to my questions and the buzzing of the city around them. I have spent hours listening to the tapes of the go-alongs in the years since. It is my analysis of these moments that you are reading. I am not telling the young people's stories, but telling the stories of the time they invited me to spend with them and of the ways I got to know them during our times together. Offering this positioning of myself as researcher does not serve as the typical positionality statement that often appears in an introductory chapter and is never to be referred to again. Rather, I offer this as a positionality framing that should serve as a template for how you will read the essays in this volume.

In line with Tuck and Yang, I position this work as a purposeful move against the tendency for research to act like "inquiry as invasion,"[30] and instead position it as an inquiry into the invader. Any attempt of mine as a researcher, especially a white settler like myself, to conduct research with or alongside other people is always already an invasion—or at the very least an interruption into their daily lives—especially with participants like those in my study who are further removed than I from the academy and from where "official" knowledge is often thought to be produced. Rather than trying to explain away my privilege and power by admitting that it exists, I have written this book to focus on the ways I am attempting to make knowledge out of my interactions with the young people in the study. I seek to represent how I am coming to unlearn and unknow rather than trying to prove I am accumulating more and more knowledge.

Moreover, you, the reader, are asked to consider how your reading of this research makes you an accomplice to these aspects of doing research with people. I suggest that those who engage with the products of research must consider how they are part and parcel of the often problematic dynamics with which researchers and research continue to reckon. Reader, this is not a callout (please don't put this book down and walk away!). Rather, it is a way of welcoming you into this text and inviting you to think in different ways about what you are about to read.

Yes, I am asking you to do some work as you move forward with reading the pages that follow. I do not view the readers of my work as unattached bystanders. I ask that you join me in holding yourself accountable to the questioning from John's grandmother: What are *you* doing here on these pages with her grandchild? How does your wanting to read this book (and to learn about the participants) make you part of this endeavor and not just a witness to it? How are you coming to know about these young people as you read this book? Rest assured; I am not trying to leave you out to dry. Far from it. I want to suggest that we are all in this together.

While our individual social positions likely put us in different relationships to this process, I maintain that the consumption of research products is, in fact, part of the research process. For all the myriad problems with research, if no one was curious enough to read it after it gets published, then the knowledge produced from it would remain hidden. Because the taking up of research products is part of the cycle of knowledge, I consider both author and reader beholden to considering how we participate in the normative processes of knowledge making by being in relationship to one another and this text you are reading.

Moving forward, I suggest that we (me with my writing and you with your reading) endeavor to look away from the so-called objects that might normatively pull attention in writing or consuming a research project. Let us avert our literal and figurative gazes from the directions we have been trained and taught to look. Here, I pull on visual culture theorist Irit Rogoff's framing of "looking away" as a manner of participating in cultural production. Rogoff explains, "It may well be in the act of looking away from the objects of our supposed study, in the shifting modalities of the attention we pay them, that we have a potential for a rearticulation of the relations between makers, objects, and audiences."[31] While Rogoff's theorizing is based in the study of museums, the long-standing collaboration between research and museums in the production of normative settler colonial knowledge systems makes her thinking useful in working toward research refusals. However, looking away does not entail turning our back to the youth in this study. Rather, it entails an adjustment of the methodological lenses that normatively keep youth as their central focus. It involves shifting collective social glances away from a sole, intensive focus on youth to instead see how they come to be known not on their own but through and because of the worlds around them. I ask that, in looking away from youth (but doing so without turning our backs to them), those who read this book resist the temptation to participate in controlling who TQNB youth are and/or can be. Instead, through the composition of the essays in this book, I hope to draw your attention to dismantling the systems and institutions that keep knowledge about young people static; I do this by writing through the moments where my own knowledge and assumptions about youth were troubled and interrupted; the moments where I questioned my research methods, wrestled with the process of embodying the role of researcher, and wondered if, in fact, I had any place doing the project at all.

Such a move to challenge the status quo of education research—to ask whether researchers ought to question the direction of their inquiring gazes—was inspired by advice I received from a longtime mentor,

Ed Brockenbrough, before I started the go-alongs. The advice itself was framed as a challenge, as a provocation to me as I embarked on the research process. Before starting the study, he asked me to consider which parts of what I was about to learn from the young people in my study I would exclude in my writing of the research. He explained that in gaining the trust of my participants and spending so much time in proximity to them, I was likely to see, hear, and witness things that participants might not want me to share with others. Brockenbrough's challenges to support queer and trans youth of color have been made more broadly, with him calling for educational stakeholders and allies to "interrupt the systems of domination that, in the absence of intentional and collective resistance, are reproduced through hegemonic modes of knowledge production."[32] Brockenbrough's advice was a challenge to me as a white scholar working with participants of color to consider how my research would utilize queer of color epistemologies to counter normative systems of knowledge about TQNB youth.

From this advice, I have kept the following questions in mind, and I invite you to consider these questions as you read the essays that follow:

- How do my ways of meaning-making based on my life experiences affect how I make sense of those of my participants with different experiences—especially along the lines of race, class, gender, sexuality, housing status, and education?

- How do I hold myself accountable as a researcher and/or a reader and avoid falling into the many problematic traps of doing and reading research?

- How do I go along with youth in a way that does not knock them off their path?

This advice was at the forefront of my mind as I completed the go-alongs, and I found myself returning to these questions time and again as I listened to the recordings from my time traveling around New York City with the young people in the study. They were a driving force as I determined how I wanted to write this book. By shifting attention to focus on the processes that went into this research study, I hope to draw your attention away from the participants as objects of study about which the study tried to produce knowledge. Instead, I hope that you will focus on the ways in which you come to know about them, the assumptions you might make about their bodies and identities, how they got to where they are when you meet them in the go-alongs, where they might be headed, and the mechanisms you use to find meaning in their experiences.

1

A Researcher's Escape from New York

The cab catapults up the Williamsburg Bridge on-ramp toward Brooklyn, as the rising sun is moments away from breaking through the darkness. On my instruction, the driver is taking me to LaGuardia Airport for my flight home. Having arrived in New York City more than six months earlier to research trans, queer, and non-binary youth, I worry that I had not completed enough interviews, that I had not recruited enough participants, and that I had not recorded enough notes and reflections. As the wheels beneath the cab continue their forward rotation, my mind races through lines of inquiry that I had not explored despite the mountain of conversations I had over the previous months with the participants in the study. The study is now ending, despite the fear that the research project, which includes months of mobile go-along interviews moving and talking with youth as they navigated the streets, sidewalks, and spaces of New York City, has yet to be completed. It feels as though there is much is more to learn, hear, and think about, I tell myself from the backseat of this cab.

Researching in New York about New York itself for the past months has provided me with close, intimate connections with the city. Sitting on park benches with youth as they pass endless, unhurried hours trying to blend into the scenery. Walking alongside youth, noticing how they interact with buildings, passersby, objects, and affects they encounter along the way. Speaking with (and sometimes lingering in silence beside) youth as the city swirls around them, watching how they carve out their own paths through the debris. This whole experience has been one long research event from the moment I landed months ago until this very July morning in the back of a taxi, decamping from the city under the veil of darkness. Although this is not my first New York goodbye—I lived in and moved away from New York previously before returning to do research here—this departure is hitting me much harder than the first. Researching in New York has brought me closer to a city I thought I already knew and loved, while simultaneously leading me to fall in love with something new—the act of doing research.

As I huddle in the back of the cab, I notice the slight pain emanating from the soles of my feet, which have endured extensive wear and tear from months of pounding the pavement, following participants across the city, running along the East River as I reflected about the research process, and bounding down subway steps two at a time to catch the train so I wouldn't be late to meet a participant. This throbbing serves as a reminder of the journeys taken with young people and the time spent being invited to experience the slivers (and sometimes chunks) of their everyday lives they were willing to share. This lasting soreness shooting up from my feet into my legs recalls the long walk down Flatbush Avenue in Brooklyn with John to their grandmother's East Flatbush house and the stroll with Yetfounded along 8th Avenue in midtown Manhattan as she popped into one store after the next, looking for a particular flash attachment for her new camera. This liminal sensation triggers memories of helping to carry Warby's belongings—box by box—out of one of her group homes and into another on the other side of the Bronx and assisting Anna cart a load of groceries up eighty blocks from the Trader Joe's on the Upper West Side to her aunt's apartment in Harlem. These memories of mobility buzz about my mind as I lift my knees up against the divider in the cab so that my feet no longer rest on the floor, hoping the adjustment will offer a bit of relief.

Out of the cab's right-hand window, the lights on the Manhattan and Brooklyn Bridges come into view further down the East River. It feels fitting to be sneaking out of town under the protection of the night sky just before it gives way to morning. New York may never sleep, as they say, but at this twilight hour this city appears to have dozed off, ever so slightly. After months of moving with young people through the city, of jumping at every opportunity to complete another go-along, of finishing an interview only to get a text from a participant asking whether I was free to meet for another, I can feel the immense weight of the delayed rest catching up with me. Like this dynamic, ever-moving, changing city, I too need to get a bit of shut-eye.

As the cab speeds down the other end of the bridge, the support cables fan quickly past the windows on both sides. The urge arises to turn around to get one last glimpse of the downtown Manhattan skyline, but I fear that doing so might inspire me to fling open the door and barrel-roll out of the cab. Instead, I close my eyes to replay a scene from a few hours earlier. Some friends had planned a Christopher Street goodbye send-off for me, a fitting farewell to my study of trans, queer, and non-binary youth in New York by going back to spaces inhabited with the spirits and souls of trans, queer, and non-binary forebears. Even as the area continues to be "straightened" through persistent gentrification, these spirits linger on.[1]

On my way to meet my friends, I ran into one of my participants. I caught Anna's eye through the window of the feminist sex toy store where she works in the Lower East Side, and she smiled and waved me inside. The exchange was brief, as she was helping various customers eager for advice about the various vibrators and types of lube. I expressed, once more, my deep appreciation for Anna's sharing of her time and thoughts with me and to the study. Moving back onto the sidewalk to continue the westward stroll toward Christopher Street, I struggled to grapple with the apprehension I felt about the conclusion of fieldwork.

During my final weeks in New York, the last few go-alongs offered very little sense of resolution. This was especially true of Foxxy's last go-along, which featured a series of tense run-ins with passersby who called into question Foxxy's gender presentation, including being catcalled by construction workers and then being photographed against their will by strangers on the train platform. During these final ninety minutes together, Foxxy offered a series of intense, personal admissions about their daily apprehensions of living as a genderqueer person. Unfortunately, we had no time to process these before Foxxy had to run off to make an appointment, leaving me alone on a TriBeCa sidewalk with a long list of unasked questions stretching out between us.

Brian's last planned go-along never came to fruition, as we failed to connect at the Metropolitan Museum of Art one June afternoon, each of us showing up at a different time. Connecting via phone later that day while I was in the middle of another go-long at Lincoln Center with two other participants, Dan and Elliod, it was not clear from Brian's explanation whether our scheduling was out of sync or whether he was trying to convey with his actions that he did not want to do the last go-along. I was left to wonder whether maybe he was done with the research project even though I was not.

These seemingly fractured endings serve as firm reminders that the end of the formal research process does not (and could never) correspond to the sense of closure a researcher might hope for as a project reaches its conclusion. Indeed, to assume that it could be so centers the researcher as an omnipotent presence in the field who is able to parse out perfect bits of knowledge and data. In letting go of the desire for a certain type of ending, I turn to Maggie MacLure's advising us to "think of engagements with data, then, as experiments with order and disorder, in which provisional and partial taxonomies are formed, but are always subject to metamorphosis, as new connections spark among words, bodies, objects, and ideas."[2] In this regard, so-called endings become new openings, periods become commas, and youths' lives keep spinning after their involvement in the study ends, leaving whatever conclusions I might be able to draw about their experiences to be contingent to the times and spaces I was with them.

As the cab races off the Williamsburg Bridge to connect to the Brooklyn-Queens Expressway, I find myself grappling with the assumption that this ride to the airport marks the very final moments of this research project. Continuing to move forward, I remain seated with my eyes forced shut in the backseat. Scenes from fieldwork move like a series of images behind my closed eyes, and instead of the previously foreseen panic, a sense of calm fills up the space around my body. I hear Scarlet's trademark laughter in response to one of my corny jokes and start to sense la Princess's focused determination about carving out both her daily and future movements through the formal and informal transphobic bureaucracies she faces every day. Remembering the joy Axel felt each time he took me to a new comics store, I reminisce about how fun it was to witness his emotion while standing beside him. I hear Yetfounded's voice start to pose a new series of questions to me, rather than answering the ones I posed to her.

Perhaps this ending I had been dreading might, instead, be just a new beginning. Although I am leaving Anna, Axel, Brian, Dan, John, Elliod, Foxxy, la Princess, Scarlet, Warby, and Yetfounded here in New York, they still have things to say and knowledge to impart. Taking a deep breath, I open my eyes just in time to see the slightest burst of sunrise peeking up over the horizon.

2

Library Time with Brian

Perched on his chair in the middle of the large library computer room, Brian explains, "Yeah, I usually go on the computer, checking my emails. Umm, listening to music on YouTube, watch videos on YouTube . . ." His voice trails off as his head, adorned with the usual black New York Yankees fitted baseball cap, turns over one shoulder and then the other. His big eyes scan the room as other library patrons type away, biding their time while staring at their respective screens. Like Brian, most of the people in the room are Black. Every computer is occupied, though there are at least two empty carrels between each machine so that the room does not feel overly crowded. Brian and I are able to speak in hushed voices without feeling that we are interrupting the other patrons or cutting through the relative quiet of the room.

The terminal to the right of Brian is missing a computer, so I am sitting beside him in the chair left behind in the absence of technology. From this intimate vantage point, I notice how Brian's drawstring backpack hangs on the back of his own chair and two black plastic bags lay on the table next to the computer. One bag contains a bunch of papers; the other is filled with snacks and a few plastic bottled drinks purchased from the bodega near his group home. Every time I see Brian, these bags are in hand or placed somewhere nearby. His phone is also on the table, positioned directly adjacent to the keyboard. He is set up, his belongings in the places that he wants them, and is seemingly eager to not have to move for a while.

Having arrived before the go-along started, Brian had scoped out his computer and settled in. This computer lab is part of the Business and Career Library,[1] a branch of the Brooklyn Public Library located just outside of downtown Brooklyn. Earlier, while waiting for Brian in the lobby for fifteen minutes before realizing he was already settled in the computer room, I could see that the collections at this library were rather small and that most of the foot traffic in and out of the building seemed to be flowing to and from the computer lab.

I wonder if the rising afternoon temperatures will drive more and more people indoors, possibly interrupting Brian's ability to continuously access a computer. Brian shares that his favorite library is the much more popular Central Branch, housed in an iconic Art Deco structure a few miles away in Grand Army Plaza right across from Prospect Park. But he also likes this modest, two-story facility on a rather pedestrian-free street, hidden behind a collection of courthouses and other government buildings. "I like this one because it's not too crowded, because sometimes the big library gets too crowded. I like to go somewhere where it's not too crowded, not too noisy." Brian explains that this is just one of his many sanctuaries throughout the city, outlining how his well-established routine is designed in relationship to his knowledge of the movements and habits of others.

Brian explains that he begins a typical day by making break-fast—"eggs and maybe a few strips of bacon"—in the shared kitchen at his group home before setting out by 8 a.m., as required by the house's rules for residents. At his group home, Brian is required to complete various chores on a rotating basis with his housemates. I ask whether he likes doing any of the chores more than the others. After thinking about his response for a beat, he replies slowly, "I don't like doing any of them . . . I like cleaning my room." From his admission I sense his frustration with his joint living situation, of having to clean up other people's messes, of having to live with people he did not choose to live with. His mention of cleaning his room makes me think about the precise placement of his belongings around the computer terminal. About Brian's desiring to have a place of his own and how his sense of ownership of space is limited to condensed periods of time, whether here until the timer runs out on the computer or at his group home until he must leave each day or, ultimately, until he ages out of the system in a few years when he turns twenty-five. At his group home, Brian shares a room with one housemate. "It's not the best, but it's doable," he confesses simply in his standard short-answer response.

Describing the rest of his daily routine, Brian shares, "I usually go to bed around eleven, twelve o'clock at night. Or sometimes I just go to sleep early—it depends. 'Cause you know I get tired after . . . my house doesn't open until eight o'clock in the evening. So I am usually tired after being outside all day for like twelve hours. You know?" I am struck by his colloquial use of "You know?" Despite his linguistic maneuver, I do *not* know what it is like to be outside for twelve hours a day, as his experience of displacement is not universal; indeed, it is specific to Brian and many of his contemporaries who are experiencing homelessness. His transitional status lasts every day between 8 a.m. and 8 p.m., when he both takes shelter in the city and makes shelter out of it.

Brian's living situation entails leaving home for the entirety of the day, with no chance of a sick day or a day off to rest his head. I read Brian's expressed tiredness not as a casual exclamation like *Whew, I'm beat!* or *Today was a lot!* but as a result of the toil of having to be constantly on the move, each and every day. To simply frame this knowledge as a survival tactic would downplay Brian's experiences with systems and institutions governing the city and, moreover, would position Brian's youthfulness through an "at-risk" lens. Brian's knowledge of how and when to move through the city and where to find places to pass the time highlights how cityscapes can be used in many ways. For Brian, this computer terminal is more than just a place to check email or work on an assignment for a class; it's his office of sorts and perhaps even a living room where he can relax.

Brian mentions that he likes watching TV when he can and, at my prompting, shares that *Martin* and *My Wife and Kids* are a few of his favorite shows. "I just like urban comedy, you know, African American comedy . . . It just makes you laugh and kinda teaches you something." I remember that a few weeks earlier, the HMI receptionist had been playing episodes of *A Different World* on the television in the lobby. Brian spent the better part of an afternoon seated in the lobby watching the show and laughing along even though it was on the lowest volume. Technically, youth members are not allowed to sit in that area, but the receptionist let Brian enjoy his shows without making him move along.

Back in the library, Brian repeats his room scan from time to time, hoping he does not have to leave but demonstrating that he is well accustomed to always being ready to move at a moment's notice. He can access the computers in this library for an unlimited amount of time each day, or at least until there is a demand for computers. Brian explains the intricacies of the computerized timer system, demonstrating his knowl-edge of the rules of the computer lab and his strategic utilization of this space, which stretches said rules just enough that he is not detected as trying to abuse them.

Pointing to a timer in the corner of his screen, Brian explains, "If that thing says you have to log off now, I log off, but if it says 'Extended,' I can stay on as long as I want." He then explains the computer policies at other libraries, showcasing the breadth of his understanding of how to pass his day in various spaces during the time he must be out of his group home and before HMI opens for the day. He outlines how, if all the computers are in use in this library, the person who has been on the longest will be given a fifteen-minute warning once a new person signs up at the reception desk. Once the timer reaches zero, however, the patron who must leave their computer can reenter the queue and wait for another computer to open up.

Brian shows me a few videos on YouTube, including one from a reunion episode of *Love and Hip Hop Atlanta*, which features Dee Smith, a Black trans music producer, talking about her experiences being a mem-ber of both LGBTQ and Black communities. In our discussion afterward, I try to ask Brian questions about his own experiences being both Black and gay, but I word the questions in a vague way, as I know Brian often shies away from talking about topics he deems to be too personal, especially his experiences with identity. I wonder whether my whiteness factors into his not wanting to engage with my questions about his race and sexuality, but he keeps me at such arm's length when I ask any question of a personal nature that it is hard for me to say for sure. I know very little about Brian, even though we met many years ago when I worked at HMI. He is rather reserved and withdrawn, despite always being one to greet you with a big smile and loud, "Hello, how are you?" He always arrives at HMI alone and spends much of his time there by himself. Besides his counselor and the art instructor, very few HMI staff members have a close relationship with Brian, despite his being a regular member for many years.

When I returned to HMI to do research, I was initially hesitant to ask Brian to participate in the study, largely because I thought he would not want to take part in it. From what I did know about Brian and his private nature, I assumed that having me following him around asking him endless questions might not be that appealing to him. How-ever, during my volunteer shifts, I saw Brian nearly every day. I told him about the project, casually at first, without bringing up the possibility of his involvement. After a while, I told him I would love to have him in the study if he wanted to think about it, couching my ask in a way that gave him multiple opportunities to say no.

Brian initially said he would think about it, which I assumed was his way of saying no—many others I tried to recruit had done the same before ultimately declining to participate—and I was fine to leave it at that. Subsequently, each time I passed by Brian at HMI, he and I would exchange pleasantries and then, just after he started to move away from me, he would turn around and say, "Hey Sam, I'm still thinking about your study. Maybe at the end of the month?" This cycle repeated for weeks and weeks until one day, much to my surprise, he marched right up to me and declared he was ready to join. When I walked him through the consent form before the first go-along, he made me repeat the line about his being able to rescind his agreement to participate. As he was the first participant who ever asked a question about that line on the form, I got the sense that he was keeping his options open despite his consenting to join the study, that he would see how it went but was going to keep an eye on the exit sign, so to speak.

About half an hour into this go-along, an alert pops up on Brian's computer screen indicating he is going to be kicked off the computer in a few minutes. "Oh crap . . . I guess somebody else wants to get on the computer," he says, as he darts his head to the front of the room. Although there are many minutes before the countdown clock will reach zero, he closes all his internet tabs, gathers his array of belongings, and moves to the front of the room to reenter his library ID number into the digital waitlist. We sit down at a table on the side of the room, chatting quietly. Brian's eyes frequently glance to the screen in the front of the room, which will indicate when there is a computer available for him. After about ten minutes, his number flashes on the screen, indicating which computer is open for his use. He gets up, without so much as a word to me, and walks right over to the computer to resettle in his new resting spot. Brian places his stuff in almost the same positions they were in at the other carrel. He then logs on to the computer and opens the same websites he had open before.

There is urgency to Brian's movements that suggests he is accustomed to constantly being on the move and that he often must move through the world while carrying his bags with him. Once he sits down and puts his belongings in the right places with his desired websites displayed on the screen in front of him, he seems to relax ever so slightly. His posture settles downward a fraction of an inch, a movement that would be imperceptible if I were not sitting right at his side. The ability to put his bags down and take up a bit of extra space offers him a moment of stillness. This moment of sitting down to a computer to use the internet allows him a place to be, where, if there is not a lineup of people waiting to use a computer, he can relax without interruption, without being told to move along, without having to drag his belongings everywhere, and without having to worry about facing whatever weather awaits him when he steps outside. Within the behemoth that is New York City, Brian finds ways to carve out this little nook of space while making it appear as if he is just using the library computer for a little while until the timer runs out. His discovery of this smaller, less populated library branch in which to pass time is an instance of his savvy, a demonstration that he has developed ways to pass the time between appointments and while waiting for the programs to start at HMI later this afternoon.

Watching his incisive, determined movements through the computer lab, I am left wondering whether his actions hint at lingering memories of times before he knew about how to navigate the city through the lens of an unhoused, gay, Black young man. These could have been moments when he did not have the tools he has now; when perhaps he did not know which library branches he liked and which he did not; when not moving quickly might have meant missing mealtime at a service agency or not getting the last bed at an overnight shelter.

Sitting at this computer terminal seems to give him a sense of normality, a moment to let his guard down and release the tension between his shoulders, which always keep his spine straight and his neck turning back and forth. Although Brian is by no means a prolific talker—he is especially mum when it comes to issues about his racial and sexual identities—in this moment of physical closeness, his body speaks for him. From my position one chair over, it is possible to read how the intersections of his racial, gender, and sexual identities have led to knowledges about how to resist the social forces he encounters during his everyday life.[2] Without implying that I possess an omnipresent, all-seeing, ethnographic eye, such closeness between Brian and myself offers clues, however fleeting and open to myriad interpretations, that might complement or contradict what is or is not said. For in these first moments of sitting down once again at the computer, Brian seems to rest assured that he will have some uninterrupted minutes to spread out his belongings and lose himself in a series of YouTube videos, moments where eyes might turn away from him, where no one, myself included, will ask him any questions.

Brian offers me one of his earbuds and, without saying anything, hits Play on the music video for Beyoncé's "Single Ladies." The sound from the video filters through the cord into one ear, and the quiet buzzing of a large industrial fan in the corner of the computer room flows into the other. For the next few minutes, Brian and I sit in silence, hoping no one else signs up to use the computer.

3

La Princess Doesn't Have Time
to Have a Bad Day

Just off Union Square's southeastern corner, la Princess waits in a small offshoot of green space, a satellite island of sorts just off the square's edge. This triangle-shaped minipark is wedged in between the spot where Union Square East (Union Square's eastern border and automobile thorough-fare) splits in two and meets 14th Street. Guarded by an established yet porous tree line, the area comprises a central circle of grass surrounded by a foot-high barrier of iron rings and dotted with a solitary central tree. Classic New York City wood-and-steel park benches loop around the grass, each one situated with the central tree as its focal point. Vehicles pass behind the benches on all three sides, both on the uptown and downtown portions of Union Square East and along the congested 14th Street. Bodies on foot move through the minipark's short artery of walk-ways and around its sidewalk perimeter. The intersections of three subway lines rumble beneath, each bench providing a different view of one of the many entrances to Union Square's hectic subterranean transit hub. The Metronome, a permanent public art installation, hangs on the building across 14th Street. It features a long series of digital numbers counting upward, parts of an abstract clock keeping time in a way few on the streets below can decipher. The clock hangs dauntingly above la Princess's head as the city buzzes by, around, and under her in stark contrast to her stillness as she waits for my arrival.

It is a bright June Monday morning. The threat of summer heat permeates the air as noontime approaches, but it remains comfortable and pleasant as I approach la Princess. She is sitting on a bench on the southern side of the grass circle. As usual, she is neatly dressed in black slacks, a simple blouse, and a smart blazer with the cuffs rolled halfway up her forearms. The black sneakers on her feet indicate she's already done some walking this morning, as does the fact that her trusty tan pumps are tucked inside her black bag. Silver accessories dot her fingers, neck, and ears; her curly black hair is pulled up and back in a tidy bun, and spanning her face is a simple layer of makeup, perfectly matched to her brown skin. Each aspect of her well-coiffed look denotes an extra few minutes of morning prep, leaving me to wonder what time la Princess had to get up to achieve this look before leaving her shelter at 8 a.m. as she is required to do, seven days a week. Every time I've seen la Princess, whether for a go-along or just in passing at HMI, she is always dressed as though she could be coming from or heading to a job interview. Her business-casual attire shows that she is well aware of the ways the presentation of her gender is tied to white, middle-class norms of respectability and legibility.[1] As a trans woman of color facing housing insecurity, la Princess's appearance as she moves through (or tries to sit still in) the city is of paramount importance to her safety and ability to move to and from her destinations.

Also packed in her black purse are a few snacks, a bottle of water, and her well-thumbed copy of Janet Mock's *Redefining Realness*, which she repeatedly renews from the library—it has been in her purse during her other go-alongs. Beyond being the first memoir by a trans woman of color to achieve mainstream success, Mock's first book frames her experiences (as well as those of her contemporaries) within theories developed by feminists of color. In doing so, she asks her readers—whether they are trans or cis—to be critical and engaged readers of her stories.[2] In the introduction to the memoir, Mock expresses her hope that her writing compels audiences to see the obstacles facing trans women of color from achieving even simple, everyday tasks such as feeling safe, finding love, and being healthy.[3]

Before the recorder is switched on, la Princess has already started to describe her frustrating morning. She has been to a government office to inquire about reinstating her cash assistance benefits, which are on hold because she was in a court-ordered rehab program the year before. "You guys have all my documentations in your system, that should be all. You fingerprint me. Every time I go to recertify or apply again, I have to fingerprint. But my fingerprint never changes." She explains the situation with a bit of irritation in her voice. La Princess continues telling me about her morning, estimating that it will take almost two more months to be able to prove that she has been clean and sober for more than the required year. She speaks in an even yet exasperated tone about having to prove to various agencies both her gender identity and her sobriety, expressing her discontent with the situation and her determination to jump the required hurdles.

Despite the frustration in her voice regarding the work ahead of her, her description of the processes indicates a clear understanding of how to navigate them, even while she wishes they could be drastically stream-lined. If she did not have to spend all this time trying to prove various facets of her identity to multiple social service agencies through laborious methods, she would have more time to focus on a variety of aspects of her own life progression. Seemingly growing increasingly irritated as she verbalizes her to-do list, she pauses for a second before continuing: "but it's one of those things that if you want the benefits, you gotta do what they say. And I'm okay with that." I'm not sure in this moment whether she really believes that last sentence or whether it is just one of those things she tells herself to push through life's daily trials and tribulations.

As they do during her other go-alongs, la Princess's words come out at a rapid pace, each thought connecting to the next, and the next, and the next. She speaks as though she has been asked a series of questions, when I have in fact said very little. From time to time, I offer a clarifying question, but the content of her streams of consciousness is self-produced. It is just before noon when the go-along starts, but by her description of the morning's happenings, she has already been through enough experiences that she could call it a day. Calling it a day, however, is not an option for la Princess. She still has over three hours before she can head to HMI for the day's programming and over eight hours until she can check back into her shelter for the night. This park bench is her resting spot for the next while, a waiting and/or living room of sorts where she can decompress from her morning and pass the time. Despite the go-alongs' focus on mobility and activity, sitting next to la Princess on this park bench is a provocation to think about how immobility is part of mobility and how inaction can be part of a person's everyday experiences. Stationary go-alongs like this one, as well as others, force a rethinking of what everydayness looks like for youth who live in shelters and often have long periods of time to move (or not move) through the city.

From her perch on the bench, sitting with her legs crossed and her left arm resting above her bag at her side, la Princess starts to talk about the LGBTQ youth shelter where she has been staying for the past few months. "It's a wonderful program. It's the best shelter you can ask for," she explains. "You get to fix your own meals, you get a laundry allowance, weekly MetroCard; it's beautiful." While she praises the program and its management, la Princess next mentions her desire for a place to rest in the middle of the day, a place to call her own where she can be at whatever hour she wants. "Having to wake up at seven to be out by eight, it's very difficult, especially for me. It takes a lot for me to get ready in the morning—makeup, hair, shower, dress."

The youth shelter where la Princess currently lives is used for various other programs during the day; therefore, she and her fellow residents have to be out daily from 8 a.m. until after 8 p.m. La Princess wishes she had more time to prepare herself to be able to leave the shelter so that she looks the way she wants to look in order to face the world and to be able to face it for the entirety of the twelve hours a day she has to be out and about. The fact that la Princess shares cramped bathroom facilities with a dozen other young people who are on the same restrictive timeline only makes the time she has to get ready even more precious and the necessity of having a precise morning routine that much more important.

"Sometimes I don't have appointments in the morning," she explains. "When I have appointments in the morning, I don't mind—I need to get up and do what I need to do. But when I don't have anything to do, especially on the weekends, having to go out here with nothing to do, with no money, just having to figure it out, is very frustrating." While time may be sparse before la Princess leaves her shelter, once she leaves, she has nothing *but* time. She does her best to fill the early hours of the day with appointments, so mornings often involve a great big hustle to get out the door, but then she has to wait around until the library opens or until HMI programs start later in the afternoon.

Time, it seems, is rarely on la Princess's side. It appears to always be in a state of either contracting or expanding in whichever moment la Princess would prefer the opposite. It rushes on in the early rising hours at the shelter and then slows to a crawl once her foot hits the pavement. Something as simple as having downtime becomes challenging for her because she can't experience it out of public view. For la Princess, the park bench, subway car, or computer at the public library become her recharging getaways.

During a previous go-along, she had mentioned an afternoon of riding the free Staten Island Ferry back and forth, back and forth, just to pass the time one languid afternoon. This go-along, which has not gone anywhere physically beyond the park bench, is reminding me what happens when a youth's relationship to the place(s) they call home falls apart.[4] *Home* for la Princess is a tenuous configuration; it is not guaranteed to be there the next day, nor is it always accessible. The things thought to be done in the privacy of home for other people are things she must find time and space to do elsewhere. For youth like la Princess, who lack this firm connection to a place to call home, it becomes harder for them to be considered viable youth subjects when it is through home (or having a reliable permanent address) that they are able to enroll in school, receive benefits, access a government ID card, and so on. Without a home, it becomes harder for youth to prove who they are or where they belong, harder for them to access schooling or employment, and harder to even exist in public spaces.

As a type of mobile qualitative interview based in participants' everyday movements and journeys,[5] the go-alongs are intended to take place during something that is already happening. The thing that la Princess is already doing is passing time between these morning appointments and the opening of HMI. She is on the park bench before the go-along and, I suspect, will remain there when it ends, but perhaps the sight of her on the bench talking to me (and the attendant privileges my whiteness and gender presentation offer) might buy her extra time to stay put without having to worry about surveillance from police, park groundskeepers, or other passersby. The go-along, then, *goes along* with her in a figurative way that in turn shows that an examination of mobility does not always involve physical movement.[6]

As a trans woman of color, la Princess is keenly aware of how her body is or is not able to experience the passing of time in various spaces, as evidenced by her smart attire. In a previous go-along at a library in Midtown Manhattan, she kept close tabs on the allotted time her library card gives her on the public access computers. She knew the timer would automatically give her additional time if no one else was waiting for a computer (as we saw with Brian in his chosen computer lab across the East River in Brooklyn). In addition, la Princess acquired a second card from a friend to afford her twice as much computer time per day. Given that she possesses time in excess but also often occupies spaces that have firmly limited time parameters, la Princess has learned how to maximize her time and efforts and has developed specific coping mechanisms to pass time in ways that tactfully push the restrictions of where and when she is allowed to be.

During that previous go-along, la Princess brought up the recent coverage of people protesting Target stores because of the company's trans-friendly restroom policy, as spate of "bathroom bills" percolated across North America aimed largely at barring trans people from using gender-affirming restrooms. La Princess expressed a critical perspective about supposedly trans-friendly policies around access to bathrooms. "Even though I'm in the community . . . I think they should very specific . . . be very like 'this is what this means,' because I feel like they put a policy out there, and you read it and make your own interpretation of it. You really have to [explain] 'this is what this means.'" She argued that enacting a supposedly trans-friendly bathroom policy does not make her any safer when accessing women's restrooms. A policy, no matter how finely or inclusively crafted, does not simply erase the long-standing assumptions about gender's rigid, inflexible binary, especially in a highly gender-segregated place like a women's restroom.[7] Policy itself will not stop women from guffawing when la Princess walks into the restroom or from yelling at her to leave, which further stresses the importance of her early morning getting-ready routine and the extra burden of having to maintain her desired appearance for all the hours she spends wandering the streets of New York.

During that same conversation, right after la Princess shared her concerns about trans-inclusive policies, I saw a library patron come out of the women's restroom across the room from where we were sitting. This person's presence would not have even caught my eye were it not for the fact that I had read them (and their body) as male when they briefly passed through my peripheral vision a few minutes earlier. It was a reading that happened so quickly, I had not even noticed I had done it. Even with my limited viewing—I only saw this person from behind as they passed through the corner of my line of sight—I nonetheless registered their gender as male. My own gendering of this person proved la Princess's point about the fallacy of policies. While la Princess spoke about the fear of being harassed when using the women's restrooms—inclusive policy or not—I participated, in real time, in a misgendering of another person who was just trying to go to the bathroom.

Back on the park bench, the occasional pedestrian passes along the gravel path in front of us, along with a steadier stream of bodies on the 14th Street sidewalk behind us. La Princess expresses that she does not have the time to veer off her envisioned course. "I try my best not to have a bad day. . . . I don't have the time, the space, the patience, the benefits. I won't benefit from having a bad day, at all. Things will crumble down to square one if I have a bad day." While her day might be full of "free" time, she does not see it as such. La Princess's intricate detailing of how she navigates government agencies, for instance, highlights that her knowledge is born of necessity. Her ability to successfully chart her way through dealings with bureaucrats, paperwork, waiting periods, and protocols comes out of not seeing any other way forward. Her history of being homeless, going to rehab, and doing a stint in Rikers, as well as her current toils at the shelter, indicate that the time for faltering is behind her.

Given her previous setbacks, la Princess knows that second or third chances are by no means guaranteed and that any future stumbles could have grave consequences. From the seat on this park bench, she repeats this sentiment over the course of the hour-long conversation:

> "The situation I am in right now, I have no other choice but to be perfect."

> "I don't want to stop what I am working so hard for because I am uncomfortable."

> "It's frustrating because I just want to get it right."

> "I don't know if the next time I pick up a drug, it is going to the time that I die."

Her words zero in on her specific relationship to her future. As she sees it, the path forward is a narrow one, complete with numerous obstacles. While la Princess sees the obstacles ahead of her, the obstacles that lay behind her provide lessons on how to navigate around and through future ones.

As la Princess expresses these sentiments about her relationship to the future, she gestures with her hand ambiguously outward while referring to "they." Having briefly lost connection to her train of thought while writing something in my notebook, I do not initially understand to whom her *they* refers. But then I turn my head in the direction of la Princess's gesture and catch a glimpse of a Black man sitting on another bench across the park. He is wearing gray sweats that appear to need a wash. His left foot is so swollen and the skin so chapped, it does not seem to fit into his well-distressed shoe. His head nods back and forth as he drifts in and out of sleep while the sun breaks through the canopy of trees to shine on his face. Moving my eyes to the bench beside his and then further around the circle, it becomes clear that a number of the benches around us are occupied by people whose appearance suggests they lack regular access to shower facilities or clean clothes. They are people who, it could be assumed, are chronically street-involved, people who actively live on the street.

As I take in the specifics of this place to rethink la Princess's ambiguous gesture to an unnamed "they," I understand her laser focus on moving forward without a misstep. The fear I hear in her voice at the thought of her potential future faltering and the sense that she is on the verge of tears could be rooted in her daily interaction with people whom, perhaps, she reads as having run out of chances. They represent the future that she might imagine is not out of the realm of possibility given her previous setbacks. Her fellow bench-mates are both an inspiration to spend her time wisely and a constant reminder that she does not have time to lose. La Princess's determined comments exemplify Cindy Cruz's explanation that "resistance in tight spaces is about learning the literacy of the street and recouping agency from youth who struggle against the inscriptions of invisibility [and] expendability."[8] La Princess's movements, as well as her decisions to stay still, are determined by both a desire not to be made invisible and a wish that her body could be surveilled less. Perhaps la Princess is looking for her "trap door," what Reina Gossett, Eric A. Stanley, and Johanna Burton describe in their discussion of the complexities of trans visibility as "those clever contraptions that are not entrances or exits but secret passageways that take you someplace else, often someplace yet unknown."[9]

On this particular morning, there is another reminder of the fragility of time. Just over a thousand miles to the south, forty-nine bodies are in the process of being identified by mournful loved ones. Forty-nine futures have been cut short by a barrage of bullets, sprayed through flashing lights and syncopating beats; forty-nine names have been newly inked onto the list of queer, trans, and Latinx brethren lost to senseless violence, hate, and bigotry. It took gallons of effort for me to arrive at today's go-along, and I had not been sure whether there was going to be anything to say or whether it would be possible for me to make it through without crying.

However, la Princess does not mention the shooting at Pulse Nightclub in Orlando, which took place only thirty-six hours earlier. Perhaps she is similarly numb and does not know what to say or how to express what she is feeling. Perhaps, based on her instant, rapid dictation of her morning's happenings, her own series of traumas this Monday morning are enough to force everything else from her mind. Furthermore, with her access to internet largely confined to computer labs at public libraries and HMI, both of which are closed on Sundays, it is not out of the question that between Sunday morning and now she might not have had internet access or the ability to spend hours online, reading the news and processing the tragedy either by herself or with her network of peers. Having the capacity to mourn can at times be a privilege. Having the time and space in life to let emotion overtake you without severe consequences is a luxury. Even though as a young Afro-Latina trans woman she is demographically similar to the victims of the shooting, the notion that she is mandated to mourn assumes a great deal about identity, assumes that since this shooting happened to people demographically similar to her, la Princess is worried that she could face the same fate. It could also be that her whole hectic morning is a result of the weekend's tragedy. Perhaps she woke up this morning as determined as ever to get her affairs in order, to ensure that she is doing all she can do to get her life back on track.

At the end of our hour-long conversation, without a single mention of the shooting, la Princess turns to me and says, "I feel much, much, much better." "Me, too," I respond simply. La Princess remains on the park bench as I move away from her into the currents of the sidewalk along 14th Street. Looking back, I see la Princess sitting with perfect posture, her physical stillness belying the flurry of thoughts racing through her head, as she plots her next move into the future.

4

Scarlet and Popeye Work Up a Sweat

Scarlet comes out of the women's locker room where she has just stored our bags, and leads me past rows of treadmills, workout bikes, and weight machines toward the mat-covered stretching area on the other side of the gym. She is wearing all-black clothing—joggers and a T-shirt—and her dark thick-rimmed glasses. Generic pump-up pop music drones from the speakers in the ceiling above as a sparse collection of people occupy various pieces of equipment throughout the windowless, basement-level facility.

Although this is Scarlet's first go-along, she and I first met when I worked at HMI years earlier. I notice right away that talking with Scarlet feels different than it does with the other participants whom I did not know before starting the study. It feels like picking up on an earlier conversation rather than starting a new one. As we move through the space, Scarlet asks, "You don't go to the gym?" This question comes in response to my earlier admission that I did not currently have a gym membership. I respond by explaining that running has been my sole form of exercise of late, and she laughs out loud when I joke about being too cheap to get a gym membership during my stint in New York doing research.

"I can't run outside; I get distracted," Scarlet replies after her laughter at my joke subsides. "See, I can't run on the treadmill because I get distracted and fall over," I add, and she laughs again, her cheeks turning even more rosy-red than usual. The harsh fluorescent lighting draws out the contrast between her fair skin and the red in her cheeks. In a previous conversation, she mentioned how being light-skinned affected the way people read her racial identity, that despite her Ecuadorian, Dominican, and Brazilian heritage, people often doubted that she was Latinx.

Wiping off the mats before we sit down, Scarlet explains that she has had her gym membership for over a year. She neglected to use it much for the first few months, but recently upped her commitment to fitness and lost fifteen pounds as a result. She informs me that she always starts off with a stretch, then does about thirty minutes on the treadmill before moving to weights. I ask if she has gone to other gyms besides this one on 14th Street. "The [Planet Fitness gym] in Harlem sucks," she states matter-of-factly before continuing, "I went to Lucille Roberts [many years ago]. . . . It was mostly older women and I was like fifteen, so it was mostly just strange."

We settle onto the mats, sitting side by side with our legs splayed out in front of us. I am hyperaware of my body as we stretch, and a sense of awkwardness starts to simmer inside me. The stretching makes me feel exposed, as though I'm putting my body on display in a way I had not expected it to be. With the stretches activating my muscles, my body is becoming part of the interview in a way that I had not anticipated—not in this position, at least.

This supine pose I find myself in is not necessarily part of the positionality statement in my research proposal. I had certainly talked about this being a mobile research project that would involve me moving alongside young people through various spaces, one where I would have to account for how my body was perceived alongside those of my participants as we moved together. Moreover, I had certainly thought through how the social privileges I am afforded because of my life experiences and how my body is gendered and raced in public spaces would affect the travels through the city with the participants. Furthermore, I had acknowledged that such forces could not all be predicted ahead of time, that doing research as a queer person who is read as white with queer and trans youth of color would involve a continual reflection on how I sensed and understood their experiences.

Where this thinking had left me as I started the study was trying to find ways to get my body out of the way lest it take up too much room during the go-alongs—at least in the few go-alongs prior to this one with Scarlet. As I walked with other participants, I tried to stay a half step behind them so that my forward momentum did not lead the way through the crowd or decide when to cross the street or where to sit on a subway car. I wanted to follow the young people's movement, not have them get swept up in mine. By letting the youth lead the way, so to speak, I hoped to notice their decisions about how, when, and where to move, thereby leading me to observe something about their knowledge of how to navigate through the city. I was trying to lessen the impact—and in some ways, the presence altogether—of my physical body on the go-alongs, without trying to ignore its effects on them. I had created quite the conundrum for myself. Even though I knew I could not ignore the effects of my body in the interview, I nevertheless had been trying (in vain, I am now beginning to realize) to make my body as imperceptible as possible.

As Scarlet and I continue to move through a series of stretches, I grow keenly aware of my researcher body in its entirety. Considering my attempts in earlier go-alongs to diminish my frame and my mass, each movement on the mat now makes my body feel larger than life. It feels as though my body is growing larger by the second—and all without picking up a single weight! While the stretches contort our bodies in our effort to limber them up for the workout ahead of us, the exercises have the effect not only of waking up my muscles but of alerting me to the fact that my body cannot be hidden.

These seemingly mundane movements are exposing the hypocrisy of my attempts to diminish or lessen my physical frame. These stretches are not making my body any bigger—I am not morphing into the Hulk as I reach for my toes, despite what it feels like. Instead, they are showing me how my body, my frame, my mass, my muscles, and my skin are already the size they are. I am being forced to account for my body and its presence and how these elements of myself might impact this go-along. Whatever slight physical gestures I make toward the supposed goal of lessening the impact of my bodily privileges on the experiences of the go-alongs do not make my body invisible, do not make me any less easy to see.

When I enter a gym of my own accord, I am usually fine with my body being on display. It is a place where, at times, I anticipate and relish having my body looked at by others. But here, on this go-along with Scarlet, I find myself recalibrating how I position myself within this type of environment. I realize that I started this process even before arriving to the go-along. Before meeting Scarlet today, I had debated (for far too long) what to wear. My two choices, as I saw it, were to wear either my typical gym attire (shorts that were probably one size too small and a tank top) or something that seemed more "researcher-like" (meaning, something that was less clingy and covered more skin). I settled on the latter, throwing on a pair of black sweatpants and the loosest T-shirt I owned in hopes that my attire would make my body less noticeable. Now, as I stretch with Scarlet, I find myself wondering if my shirt is crawling up my back or if the band of my underwear is showing above the waist of my pants as I lean forward to reach for my toes. Nearly a minute passes with my inner monologue hemming and hawing about my clothing choices and body issues, and all the while we stretch in silence.

Scarlet seems to notice that I have grown quiet and fills the void with a question to me: "Did you have a good morning?" Forcing myself to move past my bodily reflections, I rattle off my morning activities and end with a mention of talking on the phone with my mother. Without missing a beat, Scarlet asks, "How is she?" Her response is so instant it is as if she knew my mom and was excited to hear me mention her; the speed and earnest tone of Scarlet's reply make it feel like the most natural response to my statement—it feels familiar and intimate. I almost launch into a long response about the conversation before realizing that Scarlet has turned the tables on me—she is now driving the interview. This is likely both because I stopped talking as I fretted internally and because she is genuinely interested. I reply to her inquiry about my mother with a simple, "She's good."

Part of me wants to say more because answering the question might help toward the goal of continuing to build a reciprocal relationship with Scarlet—and not just because, like any good gay boy, I always have a lot to say about my mother. I try to convince myself that I should answer her question with a lengthier response. This is, after all, only the first few minutes of Scarlet's first go-along. I hope there will be many more moments to follow, during which I will likely ask her hundreds of questions about her life. She is certainly within her rights to ask me questions of her own. But all I can muster in response to her inquiry about my mom is a two-word answer. For some reason, I am worried that I might reveal too much if I offer any more.

Scarlet gets up and moves us to the cardio area. I try to brush off the internal conflict about my body onto the mat so that I can refocus on the interview and get out of my own head. Scarlet says, "Bless you!" to someone who sneezes as we pass them, before arriving at an empty pair of treadmills. "We don't have to do this very long, because you're not very coordinated," Scarlet says, deadpan, while pressing buttons on her machine. The delivery of her dig about my treadmill competence is so smooth that it takes me a second to realize she is messing with me. I meet the challenge, and volley back, "Oh no, that's fine, I'll just walk it out." Pairing my retort with a corny miming of speed walking, I elicit a chuckle from Scarlet.

As we start to slowly jog, I ask Scarlet about her grandmother, with whom she is currently living. She pushes one of her dark-brown ringlets off her forehead and shares that her *abuelita* is doing okay, having just turned seventy. Scarlet says she is worried about her health declining as she ages, but thinks their living together is good for her grandmother. "My mom says that before I moved in, the fridge was always empty, that [Abuelita] never really ate. But now we both eat every day." When I ask who cooks, Scarlet says that it is all her grandmother, who is originally from Ecuador. Admitting her own culinary shortfalls, Scarlet explains that she does not find her abuelita's cooking lessons to be very helpful. "I'll ask her, 'How do you make rice?' And she's like, 'It's easy!' But she doesn't measure anything. She's just like, 'You put some of that, you put some of that' . . . What?!?" Scarlet's story is animated, and she appears to wish that she could cook, to wish that it came as easy to her as it appears to come to her grandmother. I wonder if the vibrancy in her voice is coming from the topic alone or because her heartbeat is starting to quicken as we continue to jog in place, side by side.

"Does your mom cook?" Scarlet asks, again becoming the questioner. When I say that she does, Scarlet is ready, like a good researcher, with a follow-up question. "Does *she* measure?" This time I offer up more about my mother (and her cooking), and the conversation starts to flow back and forth. Each of us take turns posing questions to the other, as two people would do if they were just having a conversation. Sticking to the subject of parents, she asks me when I came out to mine, and I start to share more vivid details about my own life. Our conversation, however, becomes spread out and breathy as the running is taking up most of our lung capacity. Seconds pass between our inquiries and our subsequent responses to each other as we try to save our breath. Those seconds sometimes stretch out to minutes as I do my best not to force any questions. Scarlet is here to get a workout, after all.

After we wrap up on the treadmills, Scarlet moves us toward the weight area. She sits down at a fly machine and does a set while I watch. When she is done, I sit down to take my turn. Looking at the weight she used, I gather it is about fifty pounds lighter than I would use to start off with. It crosses my mind to move the pin to the desired weight, but decide against it and start my set. Meanwhile, Scarlet continues with her questioning. Aware that I am only in New York for the length of the study and will return home to Vancouver when fieldwork is over, she asks, "Do you have anything you wanna get done besides your thesis in New York?"

The walls I had built around my personal life have clearly crumbled somewhere between the stretching mat and here, and I launch into my answer right away. I talk about my friends in New York and how nice it is to reconnect with them, all while I complete my set with ease. I continue to explain that at times it is weird to be back, feeling as though I am jumping into my old New York life as if I never left. As I continue, I mention that friends from Vancouver visited me in New York the week earlier, and Scarlet interjects with a simple yet earnestly inquisitive question, "How was that?"

Like her earlier query about my mother, Scarlet's question stands out because it shows that she is really listening to me. Arguably, she has been more present in our conversation than I have. Scarlet is here at the gym having a chat, while I am trying do an interview, worrying about presenting as a "good" researcher, and trying not to make a fool of myself on the equipment. Although Scarlet was the one who wanted to go to the gym, I am clearly the one who is getting the workout.

After two sets each at the fly machine, Scarlet takes us to the chest press. Before starting a set, she asks me if I think the boys are cuter in New York or Vancouver. Amused by her grilling about my love life, I confess that often I find guys in New York to be more coiffed and put together than those in Vancouver, adding, "Everyone in New York has a *look*, you know?" Returning the machine to its resting position, she chimes in, "Yeah, slightly depressed and hungry!" We laugh once more as we switch spots, and I sit down at the machine.

Looking at the weight she used, I feel emboldened and decide to move the pin down more than a couple of levels. Instantly clocking my bravado with the weights, Scarlet guffaws, "Oh, okay, now we just getting disrespectful . . . you're gonna be like Popeye doing that!" She breaks into laughter while shaking her head, expressing her playful disapproval of my action.

Not to be outdone, I chide back, "If this is gonna be my one time at the gym in months, I might as well make it worth it!" Engaging my arms, chest, and back, I push the handles forward. A smile spreads across my face as I exhale and look over at Scarlet, who is still chuckling quietly to herself, waiting for me to finish my set so she can have another go.

5

Shopping for Stripper Heels with Anna

While walking down the sidewalk to the subway, Anna mentions that this will be a very long train ride, all the way to the last stop on the 5 train. Then she adds, more personally, "Mentally, it's a long ride for me. It feels long—if you're alone." This disclosure potentially clarifies part of her reasoning for selecting this journey for a go-along. By her admission, this long, solitary train ride usually makes her reflective—"I think about *all* of my life choices." Riding this train alone is often the only time during her day when she is not doing anything. Between her full course load at her college in Queens (she has just come from her American Sign Language class, which ended an hour earlier); managing two jobs (the club in Queens where she dances and her other job at a feminist sex store in Lower Manhattan); caring for her younger sister (who lives in the Bronx with their mom); and her own personal and dating life, Anna finds herself frequently on the train. Many of her daily commutes last over an hour in each direction. The number of things on her daily to-do list is one source of stress for her, but the vast amount of time she spends on the train going between her home(s), school, and various places of employment showcases the added stressors she faces to make it to class, make money, and make a life for herself.

Originally, the plan for Anna's first go-along had been for me to accompany her to the grocery store, but she had texted yesterday to ask whether I would go with her to an adult store in the Bronx instead. Having recently started to work as an exotic dancer, Anna needed some outfits to wear. I sensed her request as a trial balloon to see how willing I was to witness this part of her life, especially since I had known Anna from my time working at HMI when she was a fifteen-year-old high school student. Now that she is in her early twenties, I wonder whether Anna is trying to carve out an adult relationship with me while shedding the lingering residue of the student–teacher relationship, a dynamic that might make a shopping trip to buy thongs and lingerie awkward. Her text gave me an out, a chance to politely decline her invitation. She had written, "Would you still like to go? Or do you think something closer to the city is easier for you?" I confirmed my willingness to do whatever she wanted, and we set this time to meet.

While we wait for a 5 train on the express platform at 14th Street/ Union Square, Anna explains how time is of the essence during her daily routine. Especially as she invests in her dancing career, Anna feels an increased need to devote time and attention to maintaining her appearance. She mentions needing to focus on diet and exercise. "What you eat can totally alter how you look that night—it's crazy!" She references the pressure to maintain her body according to certain standards now that it is going to be on full display (and that her livelihood depends on customers' appreciation of her appearance). Her nails, face, and especially her hair are other chief concerns. She mentions that the club owner has taken issue with her hair and explains how she personally feels the stigma Black women often encounter when wearing natural hairstyles, especially in their workplaces.[1]

"I have to always make sure my curl pattern is on point, at the very least. Make sure that the part that is not out is really slick and neat," she says as she presses one hand down firmly on her hairline and then repeats the smoothing motion backward along her head to the point where her hair is tightly tied back. The simple, routine motion is representative of the amount of time and mental space she devotes to ensure that it stays just the way she wants. Her desires for her hair, of course, are intertwined with the social pressures around whitewashed standards of hair and beauty facing Black women. Next, she breathes heavily at the idea of the cost of all these efforts, adding, "Not to mention I'm about to drop a lot of money on clothes tonight!" Her exclamation is tinged with a bit of guilt about spending so much money at once while concurrently shaded with enough confidence to reconcile that this purchase will be a wise, business-savvy decision. In this moment, she seems to let herself off the hook about whether all this effort is worth it, thereby leaning into trusting herself that she is doing what she needs to be doing.

Turning her head down the tunnel toward the familiar screech of an approaching train, she looks to see which one is pulling into the station. "We're about to get on the train . . . oh no, that's a 6," she says with an exaggerated breath when it becomes clear that the noise is coming from the local tracks and not, as she had hoped, the express ones. She looks up at the digital display of train arrival times hanging over the platform and adds with a sigh of relief, "Okay, three minutes."

The Metropolitan Transit Authority (MTA), the body who operates the NYC subways, uses a color-coded system to organize groups of individual subway lines. The 4/5/6 trains, for instance, are all labeled with green circles. For the most part, each color group runs on the same track within Manhattan before the individual lines split into different routes in Brooklyn, the Bronx, Queens, and Upper Manhattan. The result is that when traveling within a certain zone of Manhattan, one can usually jump on the first car that comes; if one is traveling to the "outer" boroughs, however, the trains going in those directions are fewer and farther between. In Anna's case, since her destination is beyond where the 4/5/6 train lines spilt into various directions after 125th Street—their last joint stop in Manhattan—not every train on this track is headed where she needs to go.

The letdown of seeing the 6 train pulling into the station is not just a matter of the few extra minutes it will take on her journey tonight, but the result of a culmination of living and existing in neighborhoods outside of certain transportation epicenters throughout the city. Anna's sense of her mobility—her ability to be mobile in and through the city and how she has learned to navigate it—are demonstrated here in this everyday disappointment at seeing the wrong train come barreling into the station.[2] While the subway operates 24/7, for those New Yorkers like Anna who live in or travel between the farthest reaches of its network, the long wait time between trains makes an already long ride even longer and speaks to the public transit disparities faced by many communities of color and poor and working-class areas in urban centers in the United States.[3]

Once on a 5 train, standing among other Upper Manhattan and Bronx–dwelling New Yorkers in a nearly full rush-hour train, Anna shifts her thoughts back to dancing and its relationship to her future. "I can live off dancing. I can live off dancing . . . for a little bit. I don't understand the career strippers. Like, they really think they can strip for the rest of their lives." She is speaking about women in their thirties who,

Anna seems to suggest, have been doing it too long. She continues, "At thirty years old, I think it is dangerous to rely on dancing to support your lifestyle. . . . First of all, I feel like it's my fear at twenty-one. What if you like hurt yourself, God forbid, and then you can't dance? That's it! You don't have a career to fall back on that isn't physically strenuous. You know, you're kinda just like plum outta luck! 'Cause you broke your leg and have to live off the money you hopefully saved up. [Beat] That's dangerous to me."

In the context of her initial confession of the mental toll train rides have on her, Anna's musings here seem like more of an internal reflection of what might be coming her way than an external judgment of her more experienced dancing colleagues. While she does not express being ashamed to be dancing, this admission that there is a time limit to how long such a career choice might be appropriate or safe reveals her self-disciplining of her youthful body. Dancing might be an okay career choice *for now* while she is young, while she is in school, while she has yet to get old. It is almost as if her words are an on-the-spot figuring out of how she feels about how long she might be dancing or at least a verbal rationalizing of her decision to work as a dancer. Her saying these words out loud might be the first time she is allowing herself to fully think through these issues; perhaps it is the first time she is allowing them to move from the back of her consciousness to the front for a proper evaluation. This could be a result of the bounty of time we have as the train creeps slowly uptown—not to mention that I am peppering her with questions, thus encouraging these revelations.

As the train pushes uptown, Anna muses over a variety of topics, including her dating life and how she is done with her pattern of dating older, white, rich men; a tryst she had with her classmate that did not last long because she could tell it was the girl's first time dating a woman; how she has been popping back and forth between living part-time with her mom and part-time at her aunt's place; wondering what her father (who lives in Las Vegas and with whom she has not spoken in months) would think about her life; and the deep sense of protectiveness she has toward her little sister.[4]

The rumble of the train beneath her appears to stir up a long list of half-thoughts, repressed feelings, and lingering quandaries that have likely been circling around in various parts of her consciousness. Her words showcase a highly reflective mind, as she outlines the dynamics she sifts through every day: her ability to navigate racially fueled romantic desires, a longing for financial independence to end her reliance on adults, and the ability to protect her sister from the ghosts that have affected her own life experiences. At the end of a long train of thought about her dating life, she concludes, "But I've learned my lesson: I'm not going after any more classmates . . . no fucking more. I'm not that much of a masochist." She punctuates her words with a hearty laugh as an automated recording about watching out for pickpockets reverberates around the subway car.

After a moment of silence, after pondering her comments about her love life, I ask Anna, "Do you have a general philosophy toward dating now?" She turns her head and looks at me incredulously, "Philosophy . . . ? What is that? Like *what* is that? That is such a . . . What a word to apply that to! Like what do you *really* mean?" She laughs off the question, finding it more than a little funny to apply such a word as *philosophy* to her and her approaches to navigating her love and sex life. However, with very little further explanation on my part of the intentions behind my inquiry, Anna goes on to respond to the question.

While not confused about the word's meaning, she appears to find its application to her own life bizarre. Even after spending the better part of an hour meditating about her life in a series of poetic, nuanced, and critical ways, "philosophizing" is not what Anna thinks she is doing. Her stated confusion makes me consider the normative lessons about race and gender she may have picked up along the way as a young woman of color—that she may well have been told by teachers, adults, or society in general that the thoughts running through her head might not be worth thinking, much less expressing; that her knowledge will never amount to a *philosophy*.

Furthermore, perhaps this thinking shows something about Anna's youth, along the same lines with her thinking that dancing is a temporary occupation, something her youthful body can do to earn money and pass the time. When she is asked for her own philosophy, her reaction questions whether such a term is even applicable to her body, given the ways it experiences intersectional power dynamics. She sees her current situation as part of her journey toward adulthood, which suggests that her daily experiences do not yet count, that the life she is living right now is not *real*, or that her experiences as a young, queer woman of color do not matter beyond her own experience of them.

I wonder in what ways Anna's denial of her own self-created knowledge echoes the ways young Black women's experiences are often disavowed through whitewashed, mainstream knowledge systems and thereby considered to be unimportant or unworthy of examination.[5] It seems that whatever is *real* and *valid* about Anna's life is all yet to come. There is some yet unidentified moment when she will become an adult, and then things will start counting. Perhaps at that point in the future, her experiences will then be worthy of paying attention to, of being appraised for their greater meanings, of being able to lead to the creation of her own philosophy.

As Ed Brockenbrough argues, attention to this moment with Anna shows how "the quotidian realities of [queer of color] lives spotlight the agency of individual and collective actors as they attempt to negotiate and perform identity, belonging, and resistance on self-determined terms."[6] That Anna admits to being fearful of her long train rides, these long stretches of time when she has nothing to do but think, suggests that thinking is only done in brightly lit subway cars, meters underground. In point of fact, she is thinking and theorizing the whole day long, but her solitary commutes are the only time those thoughts are able to break through to the forefront of her thinking. Anna's refusal of the word *philosophy* showcases what Savannah Shange calls *Black girl ordinary*, or a way of understanding the experiences of Black girls not as spectacular, not as out of the world, but as regular movements through the forces of anti-Blackness. Shange explains, "You also might know *Black girl ordinary* by her government name: #BlackGirlMagic . . . Black girl ordinary and #BlackGirlMagic are coterminous. I use the former to . . . refuse the misogynoir that may seek to elide what is common to Black girls in order to elevate that which is seen as exceptional."[7] Anna's reaction to my use of "philosophy" pushes me to consider how my use of the word might be too precious, too neat. That my trying to coalesce her experiences through such a concept is my treating her ordinary as extraordinary, trying to make her magic when she is, in fact, real.

After an hour on the train, we finally arrive at Eastchester, the terminal station of the 5 train in the Bronx. "Over here it's like a whole other world. I don't want to live over here, so far from civilization," Anna comments as we walk along the elevated open-air platform toward the stairway down to street level. She tells me about the store we are headed to—a large Black-owned, women-led adult store with a few locations across the city—while contrasting it to the much smaller, white women-run boutique sex store where Anna has worked in sales for a few years.

"They have so much jelly rubber at this store," Anna explains about the array of sex toys we are about to encounter. "I'm just like, 'Throw it all away!' You cannot, you shouldn't be profiting off this shit. It's bad, it's cancerous, it has a bunch of phthalates in it. Just throw it away." As Anna demonstrates her expertise with sex toys, we turn off the main road onto a dimly lit industrial block. I ask Anna whether working at the sex store has helped her as she branches into dancing. "Being able to talk about these things to people has totally impacted how I'm able to talk to customers [at the club], how I perceive myself while talking to customers. I have this confidence. Because I'm already able to talk about sexuality, very confidently," she explains.

As the store comes into view on the block ahead, Anna's mood livens as she starts to anticipate her shopping spree. "I'm excited. I'm about to get some new shit. I'm gonna look poppin', I'm gonna look good," she says, half-singing her words as though she cannot seem to contain her enthusiasm with speech alone. When I ask whether she has a budget for tonight's purchases, she quickly says, "I don't want to spend more than $250," before adding with a smirk, "but I might spend $340." She laughs at her own response before explaining that she is very particular about the clothes she wears and is hoping that this store will have the types of clothes she wants. Anna knows the store manager, a Black woman she met during one of her first nights dancing at the club, and she has received a "stripper discount card" she is eager to apply to her purchases.

Walking into the vast, warehouse-size store, Anna says hello to the women behind the cashier's counter, both of whom are Black, before making a hard turn toward the clothing area. Noticing that I have fallen a few steps behind after taking a second to survey the entire width of the store, Anna comments, "Yeah, there are a lot of things to look at." I catch up to Anna, who is already at the first rack of clothing, holding a thong in her hand. "So, this is not a dance thong," she says, examining the garment, "technically, or at all really—because the crotches are a lot thicker. I don't want that." Her voice trails off as she puts the rejected garment back on the rack. Moving further into the neatly organized clothing section, we drift apart, our attentions drawn to different pieces of clothing. Anna momentarily laments the lack of selection but forges ahead, determined to make this trip worth the effort.

"I'm thinking about the colors that I want, too," Anna starts to explain while thumbing through a rack. "I usually like a lot of baby pinks, a lot of pastel colors, but that's hard when there's so much neon and fucking leopard print . . . This is my shit. I love dancing to this song." As the music overhead changes, Anna starts swaying with the beat while searching for some pastels.

One of the employees from behind the counter comes up to us, asking if we have VIP discount cards. "I do," Anna replies, before turning to me with a smirk. "Do you need one, Sam?" I take a card as the employee explains to me, "It doesn't expire, so even if you come back by yourself, you can use it." I wonder who the woman thinks I am in relationship to Anna—that is, if she is thinking about it at all. Although there is part of me still lingering on the awkwardness of shopping for thongs and panties with someone I used to know as a high school student, it is likely that Anna and I are by no means the most unlikely of duos to walk into this place together. Across the store, I see the other employee pointing out various dildos to a white, straight couple—or at least, I assume they are a couple. The woman is intently listening to the employee's advice while the man awkwardly shifts his weight between his feet while darting his head up and down, looking anywhere but at the selection of rubber penises in front of him.

I turn back to Anna, who is talking with the employee. "I'm looking for some really nice stripper shit," she says as her eyes scan the various racks around her. She takes a beat and decides to be a bit blunter in hopes of getting a real answer from the sales associate. "Yo, like, you know, I don't know, there are like outfits that are like *stripper* outfits, you know what I'm saying?" Anna is drawing a distinction between erotic clothing intended for professionals like herself, versus clothing that might be more suitable for more casual consumers, garments one might slip on to surprise their partner for a night of fun in the boudoir compared to ones that would last Anna more than one shift at the club. The clerk states that she understands what Anna wants. While it appears that Anna wants to believe her, it also seems as though Anna remains skeptical of the customer service she is being offered.

"You may or may not even have it," Anna says while following the clerk to another rack of clothing, making it clear that she has a particular garment in mind and is no novice customer. Not to be outdone, the clerk suggests a series of garments, each accompanied with an explanation of why other dancers have bought and liked said items. Anna politely shakes her head in disapproval at the first few. Then the clerk holds up a sheer baby-doll dress, which Anna quickly dismisses. "Oh no, I don't need to be naked." The clerk turns away hurriedly to find another item.

Wandering back to the rack where I am standing, Anna and I discuss which garments we think are likely to fall apart quicker than others. As we chat, the clerk walks over to us with a pleather bodysuit in hand. Before she can say a word, Anna jumps to reject this new selection. "Oh no, no, I need to be able to take it off really easily." While the two of them are still speaking calmly, especially in relation to the loud music playing overhead, Anna and the clerk are quickly growing frustrated with each other. Each seems to have a response to counter the other's offer, Anna with a reason each garment is not what she is looking for and the clerk always with another garment to offer up for Anna's inspection.

Uninspired with the clothing selection, Anna decides to change it up. "All right, I'm gonna look at your shoes." She and I move to the wall of shoes, leaving the clerk behind for a moment. Seeing the shoes up close, Anna peps back up as she surveys the collection. "Ooooh, these are sexy, oh my gosh." There is another Black woman, a fellow customer, already trying on a pair of shoes, which Anna compliments. Tracing her hand over a studded stiletto heel on the shelf, Anna explains to me that she wants a pair of black heels with black soles. The one and only pair she owns has a white sole, which she has already worn out in the short time she's been dancing. After deliberating over the selection of shoes, most of which she thinks is incredibly hot, Anna sends the salesclerk to the back to get her size in two different styles.

"They play the most ratchet music in here," Anna comments as Nikki Minaj's "Big Daddy" carries through the store. "You're gonna have fun listening to this song again," she adds, tapping the microphone clipped to her lapel. When the clerk reemerges with the shoes, Anna quickly puts one of the all-black pleasers on her foot and sticks her leg out to admire it. "I am getting them for sure," she says without hesitation. When I ask whether she is going to try on the other shoe to see if she can walk in them, she says playfully and slowly, "I'll put them both on just for you, Sam." We both chuckle as the other woman trying on shoes chimes in to share her approval of Anna's selection. Putting on the second shoe, Anna stands up and takes a few steps. Turning back to me, she asks, "What do you think about this place? . . . It's like a fucking warehouse." I tell her that since I did not look up the store before the go-along, I had no idea what to expect before we arrived.

"I'm surprised you didn't want to Google Map this shit like, *Let's find out where the fuck we are going.* You just like blindly . . ." Anna's voice trails off as she thinks about what I just admitted to her. Then she tilts her head a bit and smiles at me before continuing, "That's so nice; you just trusted me."

"I had no reason not to," I reassure her. I think back to her text message asking me to do the go-along here. It seems now that she really was not sure that I would be willing to come to this store with her, but invited me anyway, just to see. Her realization that I agreed to see this part of her life without any hesitation appears to comfort her, if just a bit. Before I have a chance to say anything more, Anna has turned her attention back to the shoes. "I don't know why these are so comfortable!" Just then, the song changes and "Proud Mary" begins to stream down from the speakers above. "Why are they playing this song here?" Anna asks out loud. Before I can say anything, however, she has already started to sing along with Tina.

The shopping trip turns out to be a success. Anna purchases the shoes, along with two thongs and a sheer top. Thanks to her VIP discount card, she stays within her budget for today's outing. Her clothing haul allows her some momentary satisfaction with having made this necessary occupational investment. As we step outside the store, just ahead of the long train ride back into the city, Anna's sister calls. In the time it takes to walk the few dimly lit blocks back to the train, Anna learns that their father, from afar, has bought her sister a single ticket to the Justin Bieber concert the following evening at Barclays Center in Brooklyn. As Anna and I get back on the train, she asks her sister whether she can call her back once she gets home. Instantly, Anna has a new long list of questions to sift through during the train ride:

How will her fifteen-year-old sister get to and from her mom's apartment in the Bronx to downtown Brooklyn for the concert?

Why would her dad buy only one ticket in the first place?

How will she get to Brooklyn tomorrow night to pick her sister up, because surely her mother cannot be counted on to do so?

This return trip back to Manhattan leaves Anna with more time to think, and the relief of the successful shopping trip has already started to lose its luster just a few moments after swiping her credit card. While the earlier rush-hour train we took up to the Bronx ran express, this train is running local and proceeds to tediously stop at every single station as it carries Anna, her new shoes, and her racing mind back toward Manhattan.

6

Foxxy and the Shoes of Many Colors

Foxxy is sitting just inside the busy entrance to the college building where we have met for their four previous go-alongs. Seated at one of the tables seemingly haphazardly placed along one wall of the spacious lobby, Foxxy is just to the left of the main security checkpoint, where college-age students of all races and ethnicities present their ID cards to security guards on their way to class. Foxxy is wearing a dark kerchief in their hair, as always, and a purple denim jacket, which stands out since their outfits are typically all black or gray. The rest of their outfit is out of sight beneath the table.

Foxxy sits at the table with a woman, their bodies in close enough proximity that as I approach, I wonder if they know one another. As I sit down at the table, however, Foxxy starts talking to me without making an introduction. It is not until a few minutes into the go-along that it becomes clear Foxxy is borrowing this stranger's cell phone charger. The length of the cord prevents Foxxy from moving more than a foot away from the woman. As Foxxy intermittently checks their phone as it charges, the woman seems to be reconsidering whatever social graces compelled her to allow Foxxy to borrow her charger; she darts her eyes in Foxxy's direction every time their hand reaches for their phone and into what the woman seems to perceive to be her personal space.

This was not the first time I note Foxxy's interpretation of "personal space" in their movements through the city. During their first go-along, upon entering a subway station, Foxxy sped across the empty platform toward the only wooden bench in the station. The bench had four cordoned-off seats, with two women occupying the first and third spaces and the shopping bags of one the women laid on the last spot. Foxxy elected to sit cramped between the two women and continued to talk to me as I stood in front of them. Even though they were not a part of the conversation, the women could clearly hear everything Foxxy and I said, which did not appear to phase Foxxy. As Foxxy sat there, sandwiched between the others, they spoke explicitly about the ways they are often misgendered in public, about their worries about not being read as feminine enough to wear skirts or makeup. Like any typical New Yorkers, the women seemed to be unaffected by Foxxy's words, only looking up from their phones when the train arrived.

In both the situation on the platform and today at the table, I witness Foxxy taking up space near strangers (women in both cases) in ways that I read as slightly pushing social decorum. Foxxy's determination of where to place their body in relation to others stands out to me, as it is much closer than I would choose to position myself near women I do not know in public. It is as if Foxxy is trying to blend into other feminine-presenting people around them; that is, if Foxxy is close enough to women in public spaces, then Foxxy might be read as being "one of the girls" and avoid being perceived as someone who is performing gender in ways that are too often policed by people Foxxy encounters in their everyday life. Perhaps in trying to take up space in proximity to female bodies, they are attempting to show to these women that Foxxy, themself, is not someone to fear.

Foxxy's genderqueerness often leads to their being perceived as doing gender "incorrectly"; that is, their gender presentation and identity make them a constant target of scrutiny by those whom Foxxy passes by and takes up space alongside in their everyday movements through the city. Such nonconformity pushes up again normative modes of social and state surveillance.[1] Foxxy's negotiation of where to stand or sit on a subway platform or how close to position themself near strangers in public includes determinations of how Foxxy is perceived by others in such locations.

In these two instances, previously on the train platform and today at the table, Foxxy takes up physical space near women while also speaking honestly (and not quietly) about their own struggles with gender illegibility. Part of me worries that the go-along itself—my presence alongside Foxxy on the subway while asking questions about their experiences with gender—stands to put Foxxy in harm's way by encouraging them to talk about the public policing of their gender right in front of the very people who might just publicly police them. However, I remind myself that it was Foxxy themself who scoffed at my explanation of potential risks they might face in joining the study. During an earlier conversation where I explained the participant consent form ahead of them signing it, Foxxy interjected and stopped me right after I said the word "risk." They looked me dead in the eye and laughed off the idea of risk, explaining how they thought their movements through the city would be immensely *less* risky with me by their side. The disparity between my worries and Foxxy's dismissal of them speaks to the complicated dynamics of trans visibility through which Foxxy is accustomed to navigating.[2]

In these moments, Foxxy shows me how they can deftly describe the gendered surveillance they experience while in the mist of pushing their way through it. At the table, Foxxy is eating a matzah sandwich with lox and cream cheese, the last of their leftover stash from Passover the month before. Between bites, they mention their recent efforts to get a legal name change. They explain, "I'm keeping my last name because it keeps me anonymous. I don't want to stand out as a Jew. I don't want to stand out as an Arab. I don't wanna stand out as anything . . . I just want to be left alone and be anonymous. But at the same time, the way I dress and present is making me stand out." As a person of Middle Eastern descent who grew up in New York's ultra-Orthodox Jewish community, Foxxy stands out within their religious community for having a darker complexion. Foxxy's decision to keep their last name stems from the fact that it doesn't have any Jewish or Arab signifiers.

Foxxy's comment about their gender presentation—"the way I dress and present is making me stand out"—suggests that the name change will not help toward the goal of making them blend in to the crowd. There is, nonetheless, an excitement in their voice about completing the name-change process, that doing so will help them feel more like themself. Changing their name will help alleviate the self-described "gender dysphoria" they have long experienced. The name will offer even just a nominal relief to the experience of living "in-between" in this highly gender-binaried world.

As they talk about the change, Foxxy reflects about feeling uncomfortable as a kid, that they knew they liked "girly'" things and did not mesh well with the students in their yeshiva school, where they felt additionally outcast because of their ethnicity. "I went to a school where, by fourth grade, boys were split from girls, and all day I had to be with boys. And I always felt like not one of the boys. I always knew I was different,"

Foxxy explains. Because of the sex-segregated classes at the school they attended, Foxxy found subversive ways to express their gender despite having to wear the mandated gendered uniform. "I would wear ChapStick as a form of lipstick 'cause I wasn't allowed to wear lipstick. I would wear clear nail polish, sparkly on my feet and clear on my [finger]nails 'cause I'm not allowed to wear nail polish. . . . I had to wear this very masculine clothing, and I hated it." Such actions, Foxxy explains, allowed them to express and embody their gender in affirming ways without experiencing the backlash they knew would follow if they wore a visibly painted lip or nail. While these actions did not necessarily produce perceptible results, there seemed to be something about completing these rituals that assisted Foxxy in feeling true to themself and their desires. Even when Foxxy could not outwardly express their gender, they coped by developing methods to express themself in ways only they could recognize.

Foxxy mentions having a great affinity for women in the media who express femininity in ways they desire. In particular, they adore Beyoncé's character in *Austin Powers: Goldmember*, Foxxy Cleopatra, the inspiration behind their choice of pseudonym. Foxxy loves this character's signature salutation, "I'm Foxxy Cleopatra, and I'm a whooooole lot of woman!" Foxxy used to repeat this line at school in front of the boys in their class, chanting it like a mantra and claiming their relationship to woman-hood and femininity while wearing a dark men's suit and *kippah*, a head covering worn by Jewish men. While this did not endear them to their classmates, such a connection to women in the media and popular culture allowed them a chance to feel feminine and, even if just momentarily, provided relief from feeling that their body was the ultimate hindrance to their desired gender expression. "I always was able to express a lot of my femininity . . . and feel comfortable with my body when I see certain women that I connect with. Whether it's through television, media or music, art, or women I am around physically, like my mom. I feel more at peace with my identity."

Foxxy's body being read as male (and their feeling that this read-ing is often inevitable) has always and continues to be a hurdle to feel-ing comfortable with their gender identity. For Foxxy, the experience of expressing their gender in a self-affirming way is one that they believe will always bring about potentially negative reactions from others: "there is always an internal conflict that because my body is different; it separates me." Throughout previous go-alongs, Foxxy explained that there were days when this threat was something they knew they had the skills and wherewithal to deal with, yet there were other days when they woke up feeling that they did not have it in them to put on makeup or withstand the comments or looks they would get if they left the house wearing a skirt and heels. They had explained, "It's really confusing, and it's a lot of anxiety. Because I wake up, and it changes within minutes of how I feel comfortable . . . I wasn't sure if I wanted to be more male, more female. More this, more that . . . sometimes, I wonder, do I not want to put makeup on . . . because I'm scared, I'm uncomfortable, or I just don't want to? I think it's a mix." Referring to these more reclusive days, they express feeling that being dissuaded from presenting in a feminine manner is an insult to themself and the greater community of trans and genderqueer people. That they are letting themself and others down when they give into fear.

"No matter what, I feel uncomfortable," Foxxy explains, back at the lobby table. The cheery pop music blasting throughout the room offers a stark contrast in tone to their lament. There is a great deal that goes into the experience of enacting a presentation that feels in alignment with who one is. For Foxxy, their desire of a feminine aesthetic—wearing heels, makeup, skirts—is mediated through how they anticipate the world might react to their body dressed the way they want to dress. Sometimes, Foxxy determines that presenting their gender in a self-affirming manner supersedes any potential negative experiences that might come their way that day. Other days, the thought of having even one experience where someone throws a nasty look Foxxy's way because their body does not look like one that should be wearing heels is enough to convince them to forgo their more feminine clothing for apparel that will let them pass as *boy*. I have noted such dynamics in Foxxy's clothing choices during our go-alongs. Most often their outfits featured certain feminine touches—a painted fingernail, a black skirt worn over a pair of jeans, a dark "women's cut" jacket. During one go-along, however, Foxxy arrived in dark baggy sweatpants, sneakers, and a shapeless winter coat, denuded of any feminine details. I couldn't help but notice that Foxxy's generally upbeat spirit seemed a bit dampened that day.

Swallowing the last bite of matzah, Foxxy details the pain created in their own mind and the feelings of shame, confusion, and blame that follow as they discipline themselves and their feelings. "I need to stop being the one that is always victimizing myself," they conclude, though it is not clear they know how to enact such sentiments. Foxxy is by no means alone in feeling burdened by the weight of the social, cultural, and institutional pressures that trans and genderfluid people face in their everyday movements through and interactions with society.[3] Furthermore, Foxxy seems to be speaking to the complicated nature of the ways trans people are able to tell their own stories about their experiences with and journeys through gendered power systems.[4] Foxxy's stating that they need to stop blaming themselves might then be seen as an acknowledgment that there is no perfect next step, no way to totally escape the pressures of normative gender systems. The task may be living and thriving amid these oppressive forces rather than trying to find a way past or through them.

Foxxy expresses not quite meshing in trans-only spaces because of their perception that such groups are too transition focused and their own feeling that people who do not see a gender-affirming surgery in their future, like themself, do not quite fit in. Despite Foxxy's desire to let go of their tendency toward self-discipline—that their daily choice of what to wear is an indication that they do not feel strong enough or that they are not doing "trans" in the proper way—the multitude of forces that Foxxy faces makes the experience of getting out the door in the morning one of great internal strife. For Foxxy, the act of deciding what to wear and how to adorn their body in the morning is an experience in and of itself. It involves an internal check-in to determine how they feel in that moment. Do they want to dress feminine that day? Do they have it in them to withstand any negative feedback they might receive? If yes, they get dressed in their more feminine attire. If no, they get dressed in their "boy" clothes, all the while feeling like they are letting themselves, and potentially others, down. It is as if they can only ever be too female or not trans enough.

In the middle of all this, Foxxy recognizes someone hurrying through the lobby just a few yards away. "Hey, professor!" they exclaim over my shoulder in the direction of the moving body. The professor, however, apparently does not hear and continues toward the door without looking back to Foxxy. From my perspective, turning to watch the professor stride through the lobby, he seems near enough that he should be able to hear Foxxy's salutation and that he is, perhaps, ignoring Foxxy; however, the echoing noises through the rowdy lobby allow enough of a possibility that Foxxy's call did not reach his ears.

I turn back to face Foxxy, and they push ahead with what they had been saying, determined to move past this moment without letting the awkwardness of the possible snub linger too long. For just a moment, as Foxxy stumbles over their words trying to remember what they had been saying before seeing the professor, it is possible to sense how this interaction (or lack thereof) adds to the frustration Foxxy experiences moving through the social world. Part of the gender policing that Foxxy describes is that they are deemed to be either too much or illegible. Because of their gender, people cannot make sense of Foxxy's existence. Regardless of the intention behind the professor's actions—whether Foxxy's voice fell short of reaching his ear or whether he chose to ignore their greeting—the experience is just one more in a long list of instances of Foxxy's voice not being heard.

Foxxy forges on and starts to explain their discontent with the part of themself that feels compelled to transition in order to rectify their gender dysphoria. Foxxy wants to get to a point where they feel totally comfortable in their body as it is, and they are trying to work toward finding that balance. "It's okay to be certain about being uncertain. Every time I hear that, I'm able to breathe and am able to relax." Foxxy then explains that on the whiteboard in their bedroom is one of their guiding mantras: *I don't need answers.*

With that, Foxxy unplugs their phone from the borrowed charger, thanking the woman for letting them use it. We rise together, preparing to move through the lobby toward the door. Once they are standing, I'm able to take stock of Foxxy's full outfit for the first time. They are wearing a kerchief over their short, dark hair. This accessory is a personal homage to Middle Eastern Orthodox Jewish women in Foxxy's life who don simple head coverings in fidelity to their faith, in contrast to the wigs often worn by Orthodox women of European descent. I now see that the vivid purple jean jacket I had noticed earlier is covering a black blouse with lacey detailing. Pink polish covers the nails on only their left hand. A shiny silver tiered skirt hugs their hips before ending just above the knee; each horizontal, sparkling panel glimmers more than the last. Black tights emerge from under the skirt to cover the rest of their legs. In place of their usual black boots is a pair of show-stopping, multicolored ankle boots with a solid wooden heel of at least four inches. The boots are covered in a patchwork of fabrics, each panel distinct and brightly colored.

As Foxxy walks out of the lobby through the small courtyard to the entrance of the subway station, their heels make a significant click-clack when they meet the concrete, marking their presence with each step. With the extra inches, Foxxy is now taller than I for the first time. My instant reaction is to think about how their added height makes their body even more apparent, a thought that admittedly centers myself and ignores Foxxy's years of navigating their life through normative gendered expectations and assumptions.

In those first steps through the lobby and out onto the New York City streets, I read Foxxy's outfit as more *clockable*, as making them more susceptible to public surveillance, discipline, or castigation about their gender presentation. Foxxy commonly wears predominately black and dark clothing, which leaves the more feminine-reading details of their outfits—a blouse with lace detailing or a skirt worn over jeans—less observable at first glance. Thinking about Foxxy's insistence that my being with them would make their movements safer, I wonder if today's outfit might outweigh my presence.

In what is supposed to be our last go-along, a seeming conclusion to our time together, these multicolored heels are suddenly changing everything. I realize that their added height brings up a lingering notion of researcher-as-protector that I have been carrying with me. Despite my determination to acknowledge and work through my privilege, I have been led by my understandings of my white-skinned, masculine-of-center presenting body to cling to the notion, however subconsciously, that I can protect my participants. In these first moments up and about with Foxxy in their multicolored heels, I find myself hyperaware of the people we pass, as if my scanning of the crowd might stop a wayward glance from falling onto Foxxy.

Upon our entering the subway station, both the click of the wooden heels and the timbre of Foxxy's voice grow more concentrated as we move down the stairs into the enclosed underground. As Foxxy swipes their MetroCard at the busy collection of turnstiles, there is a cacophony of beeps sounding as other passengers swipe their own cards on either side of Foxxy in quick succession. Making the descent down the final staircase onto the platform level, Foxxy is midway through a story about the day they bought the shoes at Buffalo Exchange when they pause momentarily midsentence and apprehensively glance over their shoulder as the voice of the prerecorded subway announcer drones softly in the background. It seems that Foxxy is sensing some sort of threat from an imperceptible location as they make their way down into the station, that there is something or someone in Foxxy's vicinity that is judging their body.

Returning to a forward glance, Foxxy resumes the story, though their speech pattern shifts, slowing in cadence in contrast to their speaking pace moments earlier. Each word spreads out farther away from the last, making it harder to tell that they are connected into sentences. Foxxy takes a few more steps and then ceases speaking once again. The confined space of the train platform seems to add to the intensity of attention on their body. There are fewer things to look at, less air to breathe, fewer places for Foxxy to hide. They try to start their story again, but then stop after a few words. During a powerful, silent moment, their facial expression changes as they look around pointedly and with growing concern at the other people waiting for the train.

Then Foxxy starts a new train of thought with a hushed tone of voice, "You see just walking down [the stairs of the subway] in the city where there are so many eyes gets me so paranoid, realizing I'm different, internalizing I shouldn't be dressing this way. I'm never going to be a cis woman. Who am I kidding? It becomes a panic attack. To just walk, down a block! Especially Grand Central [Station]. I take the 6 Train every day, and you see all the businessmen in their suits and women. And you realize you're in the middle and you're confused and you're like . . ."

Foxxy's sentence trails off as they appear to be unable to complete the thought they have stumbled on. They are unable to put into words what happens to them when they reach this point of confusion and distress. "What happens" when they reach this level of fatigue with dealing with reactions to their gender expression is beyond explanation, beyond expression. Or perhaps, in this moment, Foxxy does not want to go to that place to acknowledge their fear. Rather than finish that fretful thought, they wait a beat and continue: "Yeah, so, and I was at the sale . . ." Their words quickly take us back to the scene at Buffalo Exchange when they purchased the shoes a few weeks earlier.

Foxxy's inability to voice that "beyond" moment suggests a queered orientation to living and being. Queer, pulling from Eric Stanley in this sense, "is being summoned to labor as the moment when bodies, non-normative sexuality/genders, and force materialize the im/possibility of subjectivity."[5] Foxxy exhibits an ontology that, while maybe not vocalized or fully understood by others, showcases that there is something too much about their life within the bounds of the ways society is normatively constructed. Reconciliation of Foxxy's gendered traumas might not be an achievable goal. Foxxy's experience of walking into the station and having the sensation that all eyes in the cramped vicinity shift to their body is not a spectacular moment. It is an all too common one. It is part of their daily routine and seemingly impossible to avoid, so much so that it necessitates the change of subject back to how they bought the shoes and away from what the shoes are doing and the affect they have on their experience of standing on the subway platform.

After Foxxy shifts back to the story about how they came to buy the shoes, the air in the station begins to breeze past our faces with growing speed, signaling the imminent arrival of a train. Foxxy is offered a moment of relief from talking, as it becomes impossible to converse over the loud screeching of the subway as it pulls up alongside the platform. The train slows to a halt and the doors open, letting out a gust of cool, air-conditioned air onto our faces. Without speaking, Foxxy steps onto the train. I follow suit, and the doors ding closed behind us. As train pulls out of the station, Foxxy starts to meander through the car. I watch them and their multicolored heels slip through the crowd of fellow passengers, in search of an empty seat.

7

Taking the D Train with Yetfounded

Coney Island's boardwalk seems unseasonably busy on this cold, windy April afternoon. Having arrived early to Yetfounded's first go-along, I am strolling along the boardwalk to kill the extra time before we meet. The long beach beyond the boardwalk is empty, likely due to the chilly gusts blowing in off the ocean. I zip up my jacket to fend off the chill. The lines outside the iconic Nathan's hotdog stand and other eateries are steady, peopled with crowds of families enjoying New York public schools' April break, but they are by no means at their peak-summer lengths.

Five minutes later, I find Yetfounded waiting outside the Coney Island Subway Station, the end of the line for the D, F, N, and Q trains. From this station on the most distant edge of Brooklyn, a person can get to Times Square in Manhattan, Yankee Stadium in the Bronx, or Jamaica in Queens, all without having to transfer subway lines. Despite being at the far reaches of the city's perimeter, it is quite connected. Yetfounded's afternoon commute will take nearly ninety minutes. She is on her way to work in Manhattan, where she holds a position as a photographer for an operator of "party boats" that sail around the island. She wears, per usual, her thick, square-rimmed glasses and a dark fitted Yankees cap. Her hair is pulled into a neat knot that sticks out of the back opening. She is wearing casual pants and a bomber jacket. As I know from our previous conversations, she selected this outfit from the men's section. "I really just can't wait until it gets to that moment when you don't need a sweater," Yetfounded comments about the weather while moving into the frenetic terminal. She leads the way through the late-afternoon crowds, likely a mixture of revelers filtering in from their day at Coney Island and locals who live in this Brooklyn neighborhood.

Skillfully navigating through the vast station and up a series of staircases to the D train platform, Yetfounded proceeds to enter a parked train waiting its turn to depart. Pointing to an empty pair of seats, she says, "This is my seat." Her tone carries a sense of ownership and assurance that someone can have only if they frequently get on the train at its station of origin where the cars are typically empty. The seats face toward the front of the train and provide a view out the windows along the left side of the car. Yetfounded credits her Puerto Rican mother, who grew up in the city—"she's old-school Bronx"—for influencing her preference in train seating. She explains that in her mom's day the trains were much dirtier and more dangerous: "Like now there are advertisements, I guess back in her day they had graffiti [in the subway cars]." She offers no caveat to explain how trains might be dangerous today, labeling the past as the place where it was dangerous to ride the subway.

Although her mom grew up in the Bronx, Yetfounded only moved to New York City from Southern California four years earlier after finishing high school. Her knowledge of the city and her ability to get around are not only quite new but also things she has developed as a young adult. Not having the years of childhood memories and experiences to guide and shape her current navigations through the city means that everything she knows about the city, as well as all her lived experiences with the city, are less than five years in the making. Nonetheless, her movements are dynamic and well informed, especially since she now lives in Coney Island—one of the remotest parts of Brooklyn—and spends a great deal of time traversing boroughs.

Yetfounded's daily subway ride is at least an hour into Manhattan for work, and it takes her even longer to get to Queens, where she attends college and where her girlfriend lives. Regardless of where she is going, whenever she gets on the train, it is likely going to be a long ride. As the train starts to speed through Brooklyn, the sun hangs high above the Manhattan skyline in the distance. Yetfounded explains how she is never shy about asking questions: "If you wanna know more about the world, there is always gonna be something to talk about." This is an approach she surely brings to her travels throughout her relatively new hometown and how she learns to navigate it.

"So, what train did you take out here?" Yetfounded asks. When I tell her I took the F train from the Lower East Side, she seems surprised that

I got to Coney Island so quickly. "Oh, I thought the F train was local." We linger on the topic of train routes and express trains for a while. Despite her relatively recent arrival in New York, her awareness of which lines go where might suggest she is a seasoned New Yorker. However, she is not shy to admit her shortcomings and is eager to correct them. She doesn't, for instance, get embarrassed when I tell her that DUMBO[1] is in Brooklyn and not a neighborhood in Manhattan as she thought. Yetfounded's knowledge is ever expanding, and at any given moment, the edges of what she knows about the city might be exposed. Nonetheless, she talks about the city and her ability to move through it with great confidence, explaining with detail the routes she takes between home, school, and work. While it might be possible for me to see Yetfounded's knowledge of the city as partial and in the process of becoming, I cannot ignore her vast command of geographic knowledge and how she has learned to traverse the city. This tension showcases how any knowing of or about the city, my own included, is always incomplete and contextual.

Such a conceptualization questions societal assumptions that city spaces preexist their usage by young people, assumptions that often overlook the ways in which youth are producing their own spatialized knowledges against the grain of the normavitizing forces of the city.[2] Although Yetfounded talks about the city with a certain confidence as a place she has already come to know, New York itself is constantly in the process of becoming. The city is changing even in this moment of speaking about it. Each time the doors slide open at the next stop, passengers flow in and out, shifting New York a bit; people swirl about before the train grinds forward to the next stop. To draw on Eve Tuck and Marcia McKenzie, such a conceptualization of New York, or any location, as a place in the making "understands places as themselves mobile, shifting over time and space and through interactions with flows of people, other species, social practices."[3] Despite attempts to solidify "New York" with a verbal, physical, or linguistic gesture, it remains undeniably dynamic, spinning underfoot and between the bodies of would-be New Yorkers such as Yetfounded.

Yetfounded is always going somewhere in particular: home, school, work, a friend's house, HMI, and so on. When she departs from one of these locations, she knows how to get to the next one, but often only via one specific route. If she is knocked off one of her well-trodden paths, however, it is not clear whether she could improvise a new one or whether she might have to backtrack before being able to move forward. During an earlier go-along, I met Yetfounded in Queens, and we took the 7 train into

Manhattan to get to an appointment she had "near 34th Street." Getting off at the terminal station, the Javits Center Station on 34th Street and 12th Avenue, she told me she did not approve of this recently opened transit hub. Bemoaning the MTA like a red-blooded New Yorker, she lamented, "They spent $3 billion on this stop, and no Wi-Fi." She pulled out her phone once we got aboveground to double-check the location of the appointment. "It's near 6th Avenue," she said confidently before leading us eastward on foot. Six long blocks later, amid the hectic pedestrian traffic of Herald Square, she pulled out her phone again to check the exact address, only to realize that the office was four blocks further east, just off Lexington Avenue. By the time we arrived, Yetfounded had led us on foot nearly the entire way across the width of Manhattan when there was another 7 train station just a few blocks away. Had we exited there instead of all the way across town at Javits, it would have resulted in a much shorter walk. While she had laughed off her mistake in mapping out the trip, her misunderstanding of New York City's geography showcased how her movements exposed certain aspects of her knowledge of the city.

Among the go-along participants, those who have spent their whole lives in New York have differently nuanced understandings of the city and its layout. However, their understanding and knowledge of New York should not be considered more complete than Yetfounded's. The lifelong New Yorkers—Foxxy, Scarlet, Anna, la Princess, and Brian—have always lived in the city, regardless of their current housing status. They have years of experiences of moving through the city, which culminate in their present-day knowledges about how to get around. Their experiences with the neighborhoods where they have lived and spent time have impacted their spatial knowledges.[4]

While the participants who are New Yorkers by birth possess neither identical nor complete geographic literacies of the city, they demonstrate knowledge of the city and its layout beyond the spaces they access in their present-day lives, highlighting how knowledge of the city is more than physical or geographic. There are neighborhoods they used to live in but have not visited in years. There are areas they actively avoid because they do not want to run into family members who live there. There are streets where they dream of living because of memories of walking down certain blocks during their former commutes to school. However, they all still have holes in their knowledge of New York—neighborhoods they know only by reputation, subway stations or lines they have never used, and places they have yet to discover.

Further, the participants who have experiences with homelessness possess additional knowledges about how to move through the city. Their movements, unlike Yetfounded's, do not always have an ending point that involves the ability to leave the streets. Living on the streets has taught these young people lessons about where and when a person can take up space in a public park or library while avoiding surveillance or without being asked to move along by authorities. These participants' experiences showcase the ability and need to move off well-trodden paths to find space for themselves to pass time without disturbance, since they do not have a place where they can go to shut out the world. Examining these movements highlights the knowledge gained from youths' experiences with the streets; as Cindy Cruz argues, "the bodily experiences of homeless street youth . . . cannot be separate from [how] the political and resistance is measured in the smallest of actions."[5] The variety of spatial knowledges youth possess about the city can be traced back to their individual experiences of moving through and existing within the streets, buildings, people, and spaces that the city comprises.

Moreover, youth knowledges highlight how moving through the city can be pedagogically informative. That is, moving through the city can teach a person about the intercultural dynamics of traveling through myriad racial, religious, economic, ethnic, and linguistic enclaves; about who lives in and occupies different places; and what it is like to experience each neighborhood specifically through an individual's own positionality. But the positionalities and subjectivities of the neighborhoods and communities that youth pass through and occupy are not as absolute and concrete as they are often assumed to be. Reading Yetfounded's movements can also provide insight about her views on whether each neighborhood is accessible or not; whether a certain area is dangerous or welcoming, whether it is a place to seek out or a place to avoid. They also reveal her own dynamic, intersectional constructions of any one neighborhood, block, or street corner and how those constructions shift over time, including from moment to moment or from one person's viewpoint to another's. They especially illustrate the ways areas of importance and significance for trans and queer communities of color are often either ignored and avoided by white trans and queer communities or appropriated through gentrification.[6]

In a previous conversation, I asked Yetfounded whether there were any neighborhoods in the city she avoided. She mentioned not liking the Bed-Stuy neighborhood in Brooklyn, a historically Black neighborhood that is known for its large presence of queer and trans communities of color and that is concurrently an epicenter of white gentrification.[7] Her apprehension of the neighborhood is not unique; it matches a commonly evoked, racially fueled stereotype, which is shared with many neighborhoods of color throughout the city. When I asked how she, a person with white passing privilege with limited experience of New York, came to know this neighborhood as unsafe, she explained that she had once attended a dance party run by and for queer people of color in Bed-Stuy and, as the party was disbanding, was accidently stabbed after a fight broke out between two attendees. Although her injury was minimal, the lasting effect of having something bad happen to her in this place paralleled existing racially fueled assumptions about this place as being "a place where bad things happen."

The evocation of "Bed-Stuy" as a place with specific attachments results from people's specific experiences, depending on who is referencing the neighborhood and their history with the area. For some, it is a beloved neighborhood, whose longtime Black residents and business owners are being priced out of the place they love and have long called home. For others, it is one of the many neighborhoods that exist out in the far reaches of New York, an ambiguous place with which their only relationship results from reputation and conversation and not actual physical interaction with the people and the streets that make up that neighborhood. Moreover, the name Bed-Stuy—short for Bedford-Stuyvesant—is a naming of this parcel of land that in and of itself traces back to the dueling British and Dutch colonial forces and the erasure of Canarsie and Munsee Lenape peoples and cultures from this same land.[8] The current resettling of Bed-Stuy is not the first instance of this piece of land being taken over by people who did not previously live there.

A person's experience in a place can comprise either the events that happened to them while there or what they purport to know about the place because of what they have been told about its history. When a person's experiences are remembered as unassailable fact—representative of a master narrative of what happened in that place—"experience" becomes filtered through the lenses of power and oppression. Moreover, different people's experiences that happened in similar geographic locations and during the same time get melded together into one shared truth, a truth that often excludes memories and experiences of marginalized communities. The result is that a limited set of experiences then begins to represent an unquestionable truth about what it means to be alive during a specific time and in a particular space. It is therefore important to examine Yetfounded's story about her experience in Bed-Stuy without letting it become further fuel for the assumption that Bed-Stuy is inherently and unquestionably dangerous, and to keep in mind that place is always contextually constituted.

Ten minutes into the subway ride, which runs aboveground through part of Brooklyn, Manhattan's giant skyscrapers have grown closer and appear like fingers of a hand reaching toward the sky. It is as telling a vista as any, showcasing the city's vastness; all of the land between this train and those far-off buildings encompasses the same, singular city. I reflect on Yetfounded's linear movements, such as this very subway ride and our previous long walk across Manhattan. Crisscrossing the width and breadth of the city with her makes clear the work she has done to learn how to navigate its currents. Watching the sweeping panorama of this vast city outside the subway window makes me wonder about how Yetfounded came to learn to move through it. Did she first get to know the space around the places where she lives, works, or goes to school? From there, did she then expand outward to make physical connections between those places? Did she then eventually learn more dynamic ways to move betwixt and between, such as by taking a new subway line or walking down a street she had never traveled along?

Yetfounded's movement reveals what Jen Jack Gieseking argues is "the difficult work of everyday 'crossing over' borders to form alternative territories that shift the overlapping norms around race, class, gender and sexuality."[9] Sitting next to Yetfounded as she stares out the window, appraising the far reaches of the city ahead of her, I notice that she does not speak about the city as if it is that robust. She has just expertly navigated through the Coney Island terminal and has been talking about her route to work very clearly: "We're gonna take the D all the way to West 4th . . . and then go up two stops to 23rd [Street] on the C or E." The New York outside the window may appear expansive, but it doesn't seem to be phasing Yetfounded.

These geographic movements are of course concurrent with the navigation of the people and communities in those places that they travel through and around during their everyday journeys. As the train inches closer to Manhattan and enters the underground tunnel halfway through Brooklyn, we lose our view of the Manhattan skyline. Yetfounded makes a comment about "Amish people" that comes seemingly from out of nowhere. After a moment of confusion, I understand that she is referencing the presence of ultra-Orthodox Jewish people who have been entering and exiting the train since its departure from Coney Island.

The members of these communities are known for their all-black traditional clothing, and their presence is quite visible in many parts of Brooklyn. Yetfounded's unfamiliarity speaks to the reclusiveness of Orthodox communities within New York City neighborhoods, which often puts them at odds with the other communities they live alongside, especially many communities of color. While their presence is notable across certain parts of the borough because of their identifying manner of dress, there are few lines of communication outside the community. This makes them something of a visible enigma to others with whom they share streets, sidewalks, and subway cars. Even though Yetfounded is aware of their existence, her admission that this community is completely foreign does not set her apart from lifelong New Yorkers, many of whom only experience members of this community in passing as people you might see on the train and walk by in certain neighborhoods in Brooklyn.

I gently correct Yetfounded's misconception, which she takes in stride. She mentions that she does not know anything about Orthodox communities and traditions. I give her a brief "Branches of Judaism 101" and share my own upbringing in a Reform Jewish, multifaith household. The conversation leads Yetfounded to reflect on her own cultural, ethnic, and racial background: "I honestly feel like I don't have one because I was not raised in anything. I wasn't raised in a religion. I wasn't raised knowing my ethnicity, so I have nothing really to feed off of. I don't even know if I'm Puerto Rican or Italian." Although her mom is Puerto Rican, Yetfounded's being raised in California and Colorado left her without a connection to her Puerto Rican roots. Having grown up with her stepfather's Italian last name and a self-described "ambiguous" complexion, she reflects on having an appearance that leads to her being read as a member of various racial and ethnic groups.

Yetfounded's experience with her racial identity exemplifies the idea of whiteness as a concept and not an identity or culture.[10] Having familial roots within a racialized community does not prevent Yetfounded from being socialized with certain amounts of privilege because she is read as white. In hopes of finding out more about her family history and her own understandings of her racial background, I ask what she knows about her father's ethnic background. (She previously disclosed that she has never met him.) My question, however, goes unanswered because Yetfounded immediately starts a new topic as soon as the query leaves my lips.

Yetfounded seems to be distracted by the sun glistening off the downtown Manhattan skyscrapers that have come into view as the train emerges from the underground tunnel and begins to crawl over the Manhattan Bridge toward its eponymous borough. We both peer out of the window at the unfolding cityscape. Some moments ago, these building were miles away, but we are now close enough to see how the Lower Manhattan towers all reflect onto one another's glass windows. Instead of answering my question about her father, Yetfounded pivots to discuss how she recently learned about the history of film production in her photography class. She explains the development of old-timey video production: "So, back in the day . . . *back in the day . . .*" As she repeats the phrase, she emphasizes the words with a teacher-y voice while sitting up straighter in her seat, "they had this round thing that had little slits. And they had this thing called the camera obscura where they would take pictures of images, but they would line them up . . ." She continues talking in a steady stream, growing more confident as she shares information that she has only just learned herself.

Yetfounded's explanation is one of those precious curricular moments when a student voices, for the first time, the knowledge that has recently been imparted to them. As the information transitions from something she has learned to something she is now teaching, the knowledge is becoming her own, much like her knowledges of the geographies of New York City. Her words are clear and concise, even if her delivery is just a bit timid; perhaps she is worried she might get it wrong, or she is taking her time to ensure that she remembers the new information clearly and correctly. As she speaks about the origin of the moving image, fragments of the city behind her filter into the window between each of the bridge's support cables as the subway rumbles over the East River. The kaleidoscopic effect makes it seem as though New York City is spinning around Yetfounded as she speaks.

8

Warby's Lost Tapes

Upon finishing her fourth go-along, Warby unclips the microphone from her lapel and hands it to me. I hit the stop button on the recorder (or so I think) as we stand up from the Central Park bench we have been sitting on. While turning her head so her eyes can scan the vicinity to figure out where in the park we have ended up, she mentions she will probably head back to her group home in the Bronx to finish some schoolwork.

We started this go-along over an hour earlier outside of the Upper East Side apartment building where Warby works as a nanny, before walking a few avenues over to the park. As we talked, we meandered through the tree-lined walkways of New York's most iconic park before ending up on this bench just near the Central Park Zoo. Now, seeing a path between two groupings of trees that leads toward 5th Avenue, Warby indicates she will head that way to catch the 4 train. We bid each other farewell and turn in opposite directions. Warby moves away from the deceiving stillness of Central Park and toward the city's hustle and bustle; I head into the heart of the park.

The rest of my day's schedule is light, so I set out to enjoy a stroll through the park to collect my thoughts about Warby's go-along. A few steps away from the bench, I look down at the recorder and notice that it is still recording. I press stop again, assuming my first attempt at ending the recording was unsuccessful. After doing so, the screen flashes a time-stamp, indicating the device had just saved a two-minute-long recording rather than a file that corresponds to the total length of time of Warby's go-along. As the Stop button is also the Record button, when I hit it after

Warby took off the microphone, I apparently did not stop the recording but *started* it. Panic starts to clench my chest as I realize I have not recorded any of the go-along. I instantly spin around to see if I can spot Warby, as if catching her might mean we can redo the interview, that I can regain some part of what I have just lost. However, she has already disappeared into the crowd, leaving me with neither the "data" from this go-along nor a way to recapture it.

I tell myself not to panic, not to be the guy who cries over lost data. Pulling out my small research notebook, I leaf through my insufficient notes, the content of which pales in comparison to the bevy of topics we covered and the emotions Warby expressed in sharing her experiences with me. While I frequently make fun of my poor note-taking skills, in this moment there is no humor in the situation. Of the few scribbles, however, I see that I wrote the words *stud* and *femme* with arrows pointing down from them to another word: *STEMME*.

I recall that Warby had described how she eschewed the binaried presentations that queer women often use to describe themselves. She typically wears dresses, makeup, and jewelry, and I remember her mentioning that other queer women always assume she is the femme partner in her relationship. However, she also mentioned that, despite her presentation, she identifies more as a stud based on her mannerisms and affect. "Stemme," for her, seems to be a way to reconcile the two roles and to forge her own position among the gendered expectations in queer female circles.

In trying to remember how she commented about this term, however, I vacillate between remembering exactly what she said about being stemme and *how* she said it. Did she talk about it in a way that seemed as though stemme was a term she had long used to define her own gender expression? Was she matter-of-factly explaining it to me during the go-along? Or was it something she stumbled onto during a train of thought in the middle of the go-along—a term she coined on the spot? Without the recording, I could not listen again to get a firmer sense of the words she used to describe it and, perchance, to deduce her intention through her tone when she said it. I am therefore left with only my indefinite memory and this three-word diagram in my notebook. Paging through my scant jottings, I remember that there had been multiple moments in the preceding hour when, instead of making a written note about something Warby said, I made a mental note to revisit the moment when listening to the taped recording. Technology: 1, Sam: 0.

Now, without such a recording available to revisit, I replay our conversations, navigations, and interactions in my mind while all the memories of the go-along are still fresh, as if such a mental scanning will firmly imprint them on my mind. It is as though I am trying to make my own mental backup of the go-along to preserve for a later moment when I get to the "official" data analysis process. The data generated from this time with Warby is now left to memory, impression, and feeling—the ways her words, thoughts, actions, and emotions are now being remembered through my various senses. There is no need to worry about immediately running to back up the recording of the go-along to my cloud so I can be sure I won't lose it. It is already lost.

I am living through the moment that researchers are taught to fear. As I quickly move through the stages of grief, it hits me that the only remaining option is to explore what it is I am left with sans recording. The only thing I can do is to try and comprehend how data (and its analysis) can now be (re)conceived in the face of this data collection mishap. Such reconciliation involves letting go of the orientation to data as a tangible object that traditional research traditions utilize.[1] To borrow Elizabeth St. Pierre's words: "something called data cannot be separate from me, 'out there' for 'me' to 'collect,' and, with that astonishment, the entire structure of conventional humanist qualitative inquiry falls apart—its methods, its process, its research designs, and, of course, its ground, data."[2] With or without a recording for me to cling to—electronically, metaphorically, or otherwise—that which might be considered the data from this go-along is always going to be more than what the recorder could have captured.

I continue to clutch the recorder in my hand as I move between the glens of Central Park, still not sure where I'm headed. As Maggie MacLure posits about the "wonder" of data, "we cannot know where wonder resides—not simply 'in' the data; but not only 'in' us either."[3] Each step away from the spot where I parted from Warby feels like another foot of distance away from the ability to analyze what just transpired. No matter how firmly I grip the recorder, the go-along feels as if it is already beyond my ability to understand.

After taking another few steps, however, I recall Warby's voice recounting a story she told me just minutes earlier on the other side of the park about growing up with a Black foster family. Warby is Puerto Rican and Dominican on her biological father's side and Panamanian on her mother's. She spoke about her frustrations as a child when others read her as not belonging to her foster family because of her different skin tone. Revisiting this moment through a recorded replaying of Warby's reflections about the racial dynamics of her adopted family might have offered a different way into thinking about her go-along. The recording would have allowed me to listen and relisten to what she said and how she said it. However, this technical snafu makes such listening impossible, while also providing me a chance to rethink how to approach analysis of the go-alongs.

This moment offers me a chance to move away from conceptualizing recording devices as the only way to officially capture and remember what transpired during an interview.[4] The recording device is surely helpful in that it enables me to re-hear the audible parts of the go-alongs, or at least the sounds in range of the microphone, toward the goal of exploring the verbal content and tone of the go-alongs. However, even if Warby's go-along had been successfully recorded, there were parts of it that would not have been preserved by the device. Warby's facial expressions as she talked about various topics were not recorded, nor were the ways she moved around and through the crowds of people we passed during the go-along. In an audio recording, it is not possible to notice that Warby was wearing parts of the same outfit she wore the week before during a previous go-along, when I helped her move her belongings from one group home where she had been living to her new residence at a transitional-living apartment run by another youth-focused housing organization. Noting this wardrobe repetition brought various questions to mind: *Was this just her favorite outfit? Had she not yet unpacked from the move, and this was one of the few outfits she had access to?* Thinking about what she was wearing today—and what her clothing choices might reveal about her gender identity, housing status, financial stability, and so on—was as much a part of the go-alongs as what Warby said about the topics discussed during them.

This nonrecorded go-along with Warby feels as though it is both spooling and unspooling around me as I trek through Central Park before finding a way out to the street along Central Park South. Although I continue to keep my fist clenched around the recorder, the data from Warby's go-along continues to escape my futile attempts to grasp it. I resist the temptation to do an about-face, to rush back in search of what I feel that I lost, even though Warby's words race around and around in my head.

Scarlet Wishes She Was a Flat-Chested Lesbian

Leading the way through the neatly arranged clothing displays at Forever 21 in Union Square, Scarlet exclaims, "This bitch is on a budget." Stopping at a rack of button-up shirts, she adds with a chuckle, "I'm just cheap." On the mission for some new shirts, Scarlet and I peruse the men's section on the first floor. "Do you like shopping?" she asks, seemingly in my direction while sifting through the rack in front of her. Then, as if aiming her own question at herself, she continues, "I hate shopping!" She proceeds to explain that she usually gets pants from what she calls the "big girls' section," but likes to buy shirts on the men's side.

Zigzagging through the racks and tables of trendy apparel designed for what is assumed to be the typical male figure, Scarlet talks over the loud, upbeat music piped in from the overhead speakers. During a previous go-along, Scarlet shared a story from a shopping trip with her grandmother at Banana Republic. Despite Scarlet's pleading, her *abuelita* had refused to pay for a men's-cut button-up shirt and instead bought her one from the other side of the store. I had that story at the forefront of my mind as we entered this store some ten minutes earlier, hoping that today would prove to be a better shopping experience for Scarlet.

I hold up a T-shirt with an extra-long body for Scarlet to see, and ask what she thinks. "I feel like that is low-key a dress. Why is it so low?" she says, referring to the bottom hem of the shirt meant to hit a person's legs above the knee. Looking at the garment, I realize that while I thought it was cute—and that it matched my own desire for clothing with supposedly *feminine* touches—it was, in fact, exactly the opposite of what Scarlet was looking for. A long, "dress-like" T-shirt was not what she was hoping to find here in the men's section. In bringing my attention to the shape(s) of her body, Scarlet's words provide a *hip check* to my thinking, which Erica Rand describes as a gesture that "works to regularize interruption and practices of changing direction,"[1] especially when it comes to gendered clothing and which types of garments are thought to fit on which types of bodies.

"How about some more flannel?" Scarlet asks as I put the dress/shirt back on the rack. I turn to face her, and she holds up a flannel button-up for me to see. A beat passes as she looks at the garment in her hand. "Do I not scream lesbian enough already?" We break into laughter together, and afterward I confess that I had held back from making the same joke. "You made it with your eyes though, Sam! You made it with your eyes," Scarlet scoffs back. She looks over the shirt again before resigning herself to putting it back on the rack. "All right, I'll control my lesbian urge," she remarks wistfully before moving to the next series of garments on a nearby table.

Within the first few minutes of milling about the merchandise displays, Scarlet asks twice about how I am doing. She first asks about what I have done this morning, and a few minutes later about my week in general. Her inquiries feel sincere, not just a formality or arising from feeling the need to fill up space in the conversation. Just as she did with the questions she posed to me during the gym go-along, she asks them in step with the flow of the dialogue. Rather than just playing the part of participant, Scarlet's uses a conversational manner to build on the rapport between us, as evidenced by our jovial sparring about her penchant for a lesbian-chic aesthetic.

When talking with Scarlet, I often find myself forgetting I am doing an interview. Through our first few go-alongs, Scarlet and I have built on our bond that was first forged when I knew her as a high school student many years ago. The physicality of moving around the gym many weeks earlier—lying in different positions on the machines, grunting as we lifted weights, and sweating together after running on the treadmill—transformed the experience of doing research for both of us. Perhaps Scarlet decided on the gym go-along to test how serious I was about doing research with her and to see what I would and would not do. Perhaps she just needed a workout buddy and read my body as being fit. Or, as I suspected about Yetfounded (the other female-identified, butch-presenting participant in the study), I wondered whether there was something about my body and physique Scarlet desired. About the ways my skeletal shape and distribution of muscle and fat made me look and the ways my appearance led to my gendering as male or, at the very least, the reading of me as masculine.

Perhaps Scarlet's decision to participate in the study was rooted in a desire to *cruise* me (and/or my body), in a manner of speaking. Doing the go-alongs with me would allow her the chance to be in proximity to me and my body in a way that wouldn't otherwise be allowed. While said cruising may not be sexual, it certainly feels as though it represents some sort of desire for or desiring of my body. This might be true, too, for Foxxy (among others), who declared that my body would act as a shield against potential transphobic remarks if I accompanied them on the subway or as they moved through public spaces. Is that not a way of saying that Foxxy was desirous of my body and desired to be in proximity to it? As a result of Scarlet's go-alongs involving working out and shopping for clothing, my body (and whatever Scarlet felt or thought about it) became part of the interview.

In this moment at Forever 21, I start to wonder if said cruising is currently leading to diminishing returns. When I think back to the shirt/dress I just showed her, I recall that there was more than a tinge of frustration in her voice when she dismissed the garment. Perhaps her rejection of it was not that she disliked it but that she disliked that it would read as feminine if she wore it. Maybe it was even that my holding it up for her to see—that she saw it being held up right next to my own body—amplified the frustration. Scarlet would have been able to see that the garment might have been designed for a body that is shaped like mine and not one that is shaped like her own.

Moreover, Scarlet seems to be interested in more than just my body. At the gym go-along, she inquired into my dating life, wanting a detailed reason as to why I did not have a boyfriend. When I asked her why she wanted to know, she responded after finishing a set, "[You are] a grown-ass man. You have a job, you have a place [to live], you have, *you know*, the means. Why don't you [have a boyfriend]? I'm not pressing you; I'm just trying to understand." I had to tell myself to resist my first inclination to view her analysis of my dating life as a personal dig. Instead, I sensed that Scarlet genuinely seemed perplexed as to how I aligned (or not, as was the case) with her understandings of adulthood. Beyond that, she seemed to be using me and my adult-constituting "accomplishments" as a litmus test to measure her own movement toward said markers.

Indicating in that moment that I appeared to "have it all," Scarlet read me as a successful adult, as having my life all sorted out and put together. She was therefore perplexed as to why I was not in a relationship.

Her intertwined notions of success and adulthood seemed to be a package deal—one that involved securing work, a place to live, financial stability, and love, *and* securing them all simultaneously. In her reading of my circumstances, she had difficulty understanding why, if I possessed most of those success markers, I did not then have the complete set. Scarlet's implication here aligns with the notion that Jack Halberstam calls the "fantasy of future wholeness."[2] This reflects the social assumption that Scarlet, as a young person, is not yet whole, but someday will grow up to be so. It also speaks to the ways that a normatively successful adulthood is measured and understood through a lens of respectability that is undergirded by racial and colonial logics.[3] In this regard, there are multiple forces leading Scarlet to describe herself as "not an adult completely."

Scarlet's questions reflect her positioning of me as securely "adult" (and as a *secure* adult) and of her own body as something different, as not yet having reached a sense of terminal adulthood. She views herself as being in the process of finding her path toward those indicators of success. Furthermore, her recognition that she has yet to achieve them and, by her admission, that she is not yet sure how to get herself on a path to achieving them, places her in this category of *not-yet-adult*. Despite her no longer being a teenager, she has yet to fully realize her status as an adult.[4] It is an admission that she does not see herself as an adult despite no longer considering herself to be a child, echoing what education scholar LJ Slovin describes as "being a non-adult is a liminal space distinct from just not being an adult."[5]

Scarlet seems to recognize that there is work to do and room for her to grow before she will consider herself a grown-up, but that she is not quite sure how or when she will get there. Nevertheless, her line of questioning between sets at the gym also reveals an intention in her decision to take part in the research or in wanting to spend time with me. Given her recognition that she needs to accomplish certain tasks before becoming a full adult, when the opportunity presents itself to spend time with someone whom she views as adult (and as having some or all of things she desires), she takes it. Her questioning of and inquiries about my life are efforts to gain insight into what it takes to be an adult or how to become one herself.

A few months have passed between that go-along at the gym and this one now at Forever 21. Though we have seen each other multiple times a week in the interim during HMI programs, Scarlet has been spacing out the go-alongs over the course of many weeks. This shopping trip was set up this morning after I awoke to a text from her, asking if we could do a go-along today. The 5:59 a.m. time stamp of her request made me wonder whether she had been up all night or whether, perhaps, she had been woken up early by her abuelita coming into the living room, where Scarlet sleeps on a futon. This living arrangement is a temporary one before she leaves for her AmeriCorps placement out of state in a few months, a move about which she is both excited and apprehensive. She sees it as potentially offering a next step to adulthood—a positive advancement in her life development and a sign that her life is making a progressive step forward.

Leaving Forever 21, Scarlet leads the way down the block to Burlington Coat Factory. After zooming up the giant series of escalators, we make our way through a series of long racks filled with discounted shirts. Drifting past the rows of clothing at different speeds, we sometimes start to speak to each other without realizing the other might be a row or two away. It feels very easy to be with her, as though I'm hanging out with a friend. My penchant for shopping puts me even more at ease, as shopping for and with friends is a regular occurrence in my everyday life. Quickly though, it becomes clear that *my* everyday (something that is perhaps normal or routine for me) means something very different for Scarlet. Pulling a hanger from the rack, I hold up a color-blocked button-up shirt for her to see. The two-toned shirt is white on top and then navy blue from the middle of the chest down and is similar to a shirt I have in my own closet.

Scarlet looks at it for a moment before giving an evaluation that seems to connect to more than just this one shirt: "See, it would be great if I didn't have boobs, right? That would be the ideal life, to be a flat-chested lesbian. But I have these bajungas on my chest, that if I wear a cut like that . . . it's a wild time . . . I tried a binder before, and I've never felt my insides touching each other's organs so much in my life. I could only wear it for a couple hours. So, shout out to all trans people who do it . . . and those who don't."

In referring to the shirt's color scheme, she explains how the color blocking would hit her right in the middle of the breasts, thereby making them more pronounced. She knows her body and how clothes fit on it, and she is especially aware of how clothes designed for what is considered to be a normatively male figure will fit her. If she were flat-chested, the shirt would hang flat on her body rather than have the point where the color changes lay right over her torso, signaling that the shirt was not devised to fit a body shaped like her own. Her wish to be a "flat-chested lesbian" shows her longing for her body to be different without necessarily signaling the need to transition genders. It also points to the limitations of "lesbian" as a signifier with specific racial and classed connotations.

To borrow the words of Gloria Anzaldúa: "the term lesbian *es problemón*"[6] (it's a problem). Scarlet's experimentation with a binder—she shared with me that she once borrowed a friend's—led her to conclude that dealing with her breasts is more desirable than trying to modify her body to hide them, whether temporarily or permanently. Further, she recognizes the hardships experienced by (while also distinguishing herself from) both trans guys who bind and trans guys who do not. Regardless of the words Scarlet uses to describe herself—*lesbian, not complete adult*—they are always incomplete, always imperfect. Scarlet's expression of her gender identity can be considered alongside those other markers of how she envisions her future (and hopefully successful) adult self, meaning that her womanness is part of how she sees her fully realized self once she crosses the threshold into adulthood. In this moment, her words indicate her identity as *lesbian* (and *woman*) despite her wish for more manageable breasts (or perhaps the means to access affordable clothing that would accentuate her body in the way she desires). Scarlet's positioning of herself highlights how *cis* as a term to imply "not trans" showcases the limits in both terms while also showing that "cisness" is only ever understood through successfully presented normative ideals of whiteness and adulthood.[7]

When Scarlet had the chance to select her own pseudonym for the study, I wondered whether she would take this opportunity for a new form of representation away from her actual name, which was one highly associated with normative cultural representations of womanhood, femininity, and motherhood. Her selection of "Scarlet" as a pseudonym, however, did not avoid her representation as being caught up with cultural signifiers of "woman." Its utterance triggers particularly gendered images—for instance, the consummate Southern belle, Scarlett O'Hara, from *Gone with the Wind* or the exemplification of female immorality in *The Scarlet Letter*.

However, her selection of the name "Scarlet" reflects a specific desire to resist normative senses of binaried gender, whether intentionally or not. Regardless of Scarlet's gender identity, her body is often read as not aligning with gender norms, and she experiences her body in relation to the world in ways that signify she is transgressive. She may not call herself genderqueer, but she is certainly queering gender, her experiences with gym locker rooms serving as a prime example. During the gym go-along, Scarlet told me she often stares down women in the women's locker room who give her body concerned looks, wondering whether she is in the wrong facility. She also related an experience she had with her trans guy friend: when they used the men's locker room together, it was Scarlet (and not her friend) who took the lead in explaining to the manager why he was wrong to confront the pair and question their use of the facility. In one scenario, Scarlet is standing up for the fact that gender presentation does not make her less entitled to the women's room. In another, she is doing the double-pronged work of being an ally for her trans friend in advocating for his right to use the men's room while simultaneously challenging the gender segregation of facilities altogether by using the men's room herself.

In a similar manner, her selection of Scarlet suggests a desire to remain in a position that refuses a normative sense of "cohesion" among gender expression, presentation, and identity.[8] She can call herself Scarlet while embodying a masculine presentation. Most important, all this positioning on her part should not be considered part of a youthful exploration, regardless of whether or not it shifts with the passing of time. Where she is in this moment with her gender identity, expression, and presentation does not become invalid as she "grows up," regardless of whether her presentation or identification changes over time. Her current consideration of how she views her body and identity in relation to the world lands her within organizing schema of gender and sex and should be validated, not questioned as being part of some sort of partial or fleeting stop on her journey of and through gender.

In theorizing about youth and their experiences of expressing and embodying gender, we must avoid the supposition that young people are allowed, to an extent, to experiment with identity and presentation, as long as said exploration solidifies once they reach adulthood.[9] The view of identity formation as an exclusively youthful endeavor implies that a shift in an adult's gender presentation might indicate that they are not who they were before the shift, that adults should already know who they are. This notion stems from a form of discipline that exists even within some frames that are inclusive of queer and trans experiences.

This is important for understanding Scarlet's experiences as "real" and "valid," even as she sorts out what being adult might look like. To take seriously her experiences, one must resist the tendency to speculate about where her presentation and expression might be headed and instead appraise what she is doing in the moment. In this light, Scarlet's multifaceted determinations of how to move through the world as a gendered being—even with the subsequent frustration she experiences, such as the trouble finding clothes she likes—show a keen sense of how she has learned to navigate and exist within the world around her.

While waiting in the checkout line at Burlington Coat Factory with the one shirt she found to buy, Scarlet explains, "I realized a long time ago, if I listen to everything they say, my life would be different—but not for the better." In this case she is referring to her family (mainly, her mother and abuelita), but the lesson has wider ramifications. She is not saying she does not listen to *anything* her family says, because, as is the case with pervasive gender norms, it is impossible to live outside of the disciplinary systems that shape the social worlds within which she exists. However, she does indicate that she does not listen to *everything* they say. She has developed a system for deciding when and how not to abide by her mother and grandmother's expectations of her, as well as when and how she subverts or adheres to the administration of gender rules from whichever source they come.

Finishing her purchase, she turns to me and says, "I think we should go to the Goodwill . . ." Punctuating her statement with a smile, as usual, she adds, ". . . with my broke ass!" Our laughter echoes down the escalator as we make our way out to 14th Street.

10

To Grandmother's House John Goes

Just a few moments into the go-along, John asks, "Can we walk slower?" Even though I started the go-along with the intention of walking slowly so as to let John set the pace, my efforts do not seem to have sufficed. As we continue to move down Church Avenue in Brooklyn, the difference in our walking strides starts to highlight other differences between us. I wonder how we are read when walking together, me an adult white man and John a Black teenage gender-fluid person who is often read as, and assumed to be, female. John expresses their gender fluidity visually in ways that are often imperceptible to an unknowing eye. On a previous go-along they mentioned wearing their sweatshirt hood over their head as one example of how they present when feeling more masculine. Today, John is walking me through East Flatbush, a predominately Black and West Indian neighborhood in Central Brooklyn. The active sidewalks are lined with pedestrians, almost all of color, filtering in and out of businesses. We pass through several groups of young people of color, presumably just leaving one of the schools in the surrounding area.

John begins to explain that they are having some trouble at school: "I'm in danger of not graduating, as embarrassing as it is to say." John's guidance counselor called them last week to explain that John needed to do extra work by the following week to get their grades up in order to pass. After checking in with their teachers, John is not convinced that they are taking John's request seriously. Confessing to currently having a 12 percent in their math class, John explains that their math teacher provided only one extra assignment. While math has always been their "worst subject ever," John incredulously explains their suspicions that the teachers are not doing enough to ensure that John will be able to graduate.

"It was frustrating when I was like, 'Are you taking this seriously? Like, is this a joke? . . .' [The math teacher] kinda had a flippant attitude, and I was like, 'C'mon man, I'm trying to graduate. You know I'm a good kid!'" With John's reference to the notion of being a "good kid," I see a connection to their awareness that certain constructions of youth are aligned with positive attributes and others with negative ones.[1] In this regard, it is beneficial to John's well-being to be known as a "good kid" or good student. In trying to prove themself to be a worthwhile student, John is working against the normative habits of thought controlled by hetero and cisgender normativity[2] and whiteness,[3] which pathologize certain experiences of queer, trans, and racialized students. John then lets out a long sigh and, after a beat, adds, "I would have felt better if he'd given me a mountain of work." Having already been accepted to one of the two-year colleges in the City University of New York (CUNY) system for the fall, John would be disappointed by such a setback.

Passing the street where John's boyfriend lives, John points down the block to gesture toward his apartment complex. Recently, there was a period when John was not allowed to visit him. "His mom saw us cuddling," John explains. "I like to be very proper . . . when it comes to being around his mom and being in public, in general, so I didn't think that the cuddling was a problem. But I guess she saw that, and she was just not comfortable." John had recently smoothed things over with the mother and was now allowed, once again, to visit the apartment. "He just has to ask [his mother], and she'll usually say yes, unless I was just over the other day." When I mention how I imagine that many young people do not have a place they can hang out with a partner, especially a place where they are free to be affectionate and intimate, John immediately nods their head in affirmation. "Yeah, it sucks! It sucks. It sucks. It sucks. Especially places that are free and cheap. Like you can't go to the movies all the time because you know in New York it's like forty bucks, not including food."

A McDonald's across the street prompts John to admit that they wanted a McFlurry but knew their boyfriend would be mad if they had one. After I ask why, John looks at me with a facial expression that indicates either that I had missed something big or that they had failed to disclose something significant. "Oh . . . ," they exclaimed, with a bit of surprise that I did not know already the answer and, perhaps, a bit apprehensive about having to explain, not sure how I would respond. "Are you aware of BDSM? You're aware of, like, sometimes if you're in a consensual BSDM relationship, you get rules and guidelines and stuff. So, it's not heavy BDSM, but if I know he wouldn't want me to do something, I don't do it."

John goes on to explain the guidelines they have set out for their relationship. While John had experience exploring BDSM dynamics with an ex-girlfriend in Florida, it is new to their boyfriend and something John has been encouraging him to explore further throughout their six-month-long relationship. "I don't call him Master or Sir, but the framework is there," they explain, implying that while their "Dom/sub" dynamics may not always be visible, there is an understanding of the roles they play in the relationship and that they come from a place of respect and trust. Going on, John adds, "And it's very equal. Like I can't lie, but he can't also lie." John's boyfriend, according to John, is stronger willed and more able to focus on achieving goals, characteristics that John wishes they possessed. They express how their BDSM principles help them move in that direction. Through practicing BDSM, John can better understand their own self. John's engagement in BDSM, then, has educational potential to assist them in better understanding themself and how they relate to others.[4] Through these experiments in relationship building, John is able to demonstrate how their experiences produce knowledge.

We walk down a long stretch of Church and then Flatbush Avenues. Something on each block prompts John to change topic, their attention drawn here or there by the surroundings. "You know, I never walk, never walk home. Usually, I take the train," John confesses very matter-of-factly a while later. They explain that, having grown up in Florida, they are used to driving everywhere. "My mom used to drive us to the mailbox," John says to prove their point. This disclosure comes after almost forty-five minutes of meandering side by side on the way to their grandmother's house, where John currently lives.

Although it was John who made the original decision to walk home, their declaration halfway through the go-along acknowledges that this journey breaks the cardinal rule outlined by the research project—that the person conducting the go-alongs is supposed to *go along* with something the participant would have already been doing. The project's focus on participants' everyday experiences makes go-alongs an important method, as they purportedly offer access to commonplace events and moments in young people's lives by enabling me, as researcher, to be with them as they experience the quotidian aspects of daily life, aspects that they may not think to mention in a traditional interview.[5] While the go-along is an appealing methodology, which aligns with certain theoretical tenets of this project, it is not without its limitations. Namely, this project is designed around the concession that my presence in young people's everyday movements will, in fact, make those movements *not* everyday because of whatever specific reverberations my body has on the participants' movements through the spaces they travel.

Readings of my whiteness and maleness, for instance, stand to provide a certain amount of cover when participants and I travel together through spaces where participants often find themselves under surveillance by various administrative forces. Foxxy, among others, told me this directly. This sentiment highlights how my body is allowed to move through space in privileged ways and that moving through the city with me might allow participants to siphon off a bit of that privilege. Moving around the city with me might prevent a sideways glare or catcall from being directed their way, allow them extra time on a park bench before being asked to move along, or extend them the ability to enter certain businesses without being tailed by an employee. On the other hand, my presence has the potential to draw attention to the bodies of youth of color while moving through neighborhoods where my racialization makes me an outlier, where my being read as white might draw more eyes to the young people. As we are currently walking through East Flatbush sidewalks populated almost exclusively by Black and Brown people, John tells me, "I feel like I didn't grow up in a culturally Black neighborhood, but now I'm completely immersed in it." I find myself scanning the people around us to try to sense whether anyone else is noticing my whiteness.

"I'll definitely take you up to my door, so you can see my house. I think it's a pretty rad house," John says as we continue down the block. It hits me that this will be one of very few go-alongs completed near a participant's home or even in the neighborhood where they live. It stands to reason that my going along with youth into communities composed predominately of people of color could draw unwanted attention to them. For trans and non-binary participants especially, this might add to the gendered scrutiny they experience every day from passersby.

In thinking about the many youth who declined to participate in the study after I tried to recruit them, I can't possibly know beyond speculation their reasons for not wanting to be involved. However, since participating in the study would involve young people letting me into their lives in very personal ways, I imagine that the youth who declined to participate might have based their decision on not wanting to have someone move with them through the city. Having someone be witness to their everyday journeys and experiences could have seemed too personally infringing. Perhaps there was something about me specifically that made them feel uncomfortable or unsure about participating.

Moreover, for the youth who did elect to participate in inviting me into their everyday lives, there have been multiple examples of how their consenting to participate appeared to be a transactional decision—they wanted or intended to get something out of their participation. Scarlet and Yetfounded both spent a great deal of their go-alongs asking me questions about my life and experiences, and exhibited a sincere desire to hear my opinion about a variety of topics. Their inquiries into my own thinking suggested that they wanted something out of these go-alongs, that while recognizing that they were the subjects of this research project, they also believed they could and should receive something in return for opening up their lives for the sake of research. Further, their actions reflected their inquisitive nature and showed how they learned about the worlds around them and how to move through them.

For Warby's third go-along, we met at a café close to her job. I ate lunch and worked on an article while waiting for Warby to finish her shift. My intention was that we would leave the café when she arrived. After thirty minutes of talking, it hit me that we had not moved from the spot I picked out and that we were breaking the one rule I had for the go-alongs—that they should involve doing something the youth would already be doing in their daily lives. Sitting in that café was not part of Warby's everyday experience, as, upon arriving, she mentioned she had never been to the café, though she worked around the corner. At one point, she expressed considerable sticker shock at the price of the food on the menu, prompting me to sheepishly crumple up the receipt from my lunch lying on the table between us. When I asked Warby what she would have done if we had not planned to meet that afternoon, she explained she would have just taken the train home. As we continued talking, I started to wonder whether she was perhaps trying to use the study for her own purposes, to have a break from her everyday routines. While I tried to suggest we move and that she lead me to whatever it was she was going to do next, Warby brushed off my proposition, seeming very content to remain at the café. We stayed put for the next ninety minutes.

In today's go-along with John, their decision to walk home from the appointment at the hospital seems to be based on the fact of my presence. Perhaps it is happenstance or nice weather or a desire to clear their head after talking to their psychiatrist that leads them to decide to take this walk home, seemingly for the first time. Or perhaps having a companion for the journey has given John the sense of security to use the go-along as a chance to break from their everyday routine by walking home to explore their still relatively new neighborhood.

Hearing John talk about what they usually do without me compared to what they are doing on this go-along with me causes me to reflect on what it is like for them to navigate through public space as a Black, genderfluid young person.[6] Trying to research the everyday is an ever-moving target when accounting for the impact that participation in this study has on participants' daily routines and actions. Nevertheless, the commitment to focusing on the everyday—and the subsequent choice of the go-alongs as a method to maintain this analytical focus—entails attempting to think differently about youths' movements rather than attempting to uncover some aspect of *truth* in everyday moments.

Although, like John, I lack familiarity with the East Flatbush neighborhood, my relative knowledge of Brooklyn geography leads me to suspect that we aren't taking the most direct route to John's house and instead are making a rather arched loop through this neighborhood. I deduce from John's comments that we are walking along the bus route that they usually take to get to and from school, rather than walking the more direct route via the side streets to John's grandmother's house. Staying on major streets, which are heavily trafficked with pedestrians and bus routes and lined with well-patronized stores and restaurants, emphasizes John's echoing of their grandmother's warning about avoiding other parts of the neighborhood considered to be more dangerous.

Along the way, John points out places they know and patronize: their boyfriend's apartment; their high school; where they catch the bus; the library they like, but cannot visit because they have too many overdue fines; the Chinese restaurant they like, the Chinese restaurant they used to like, but now like less because they found the other one; and many others. These declarations seem to thread space together for John as they point to one storefront after another after another. As they tell me about them, the geographic relationship between the various places is coalescing in their mind, echoing what Sarah Pink explains as the way social subjects "are involved in a continuous process of emplaced engagement with the material, sensory, social and cultural contexts in which we dwell."[7] John's knowledge of the neighborhood seems to be becoming concrete, or at least firming up bit by bit, as they speak about their surroundings while in motion themself.

Before turning off the main road and onto a residential side street, John points to where they usually get off the bus to walk the remaining blocks home to their grandmother's house. "This is an area I know really well," John explains, a confession that seems to imply they are unfamiliar with the areas we just passed through even though John spent the past hour constantly pointing out businesses and landmarks with which they seem intimately acquainted. As we round the corner, the dwindling of the traffic noises and hustle and bustle of the sidewalk behind us appears to induce an ounce of relaxation in John's body, and they let out a few sighs.

"We're about home," they comment, signaling that the road ahead is a bit more familiar than the road behind. This seems to be the part of their daily commute on foot, the space between where they live and the nearest public transit routes. They reflect, "I'm very glad I walked. This is very healthy . . . I should do this more often." John looks down to answer a text message as we approach a corner. When they start to lean forward without looking as if to move into the crosswalk despite the oncoming traffic, I instantly grab their arm to pull them back. "Sorry," I say while pointing to the red Don't Walk signal across the street to justify my unexpected touch of their body. "No problem. I appreciate it, 'cause I probably would have kept on walking," John replies with a half chuckle as we wait for the light to change.

On the next block, we pass a humble, red-brick church with a thick growth of ivy swallowing the entire corner of the edifice. Struck by the sight, I stop walking and notice how the slight wind in the air creates the illusion that the leaves are actively cascading along the bricks. John stops and follows my eyes upward. "That's beautiful! I wonder how it's doing that," they remark with awe. The two of us take a moment to appreciate the green waterfall of ivy pouring down the side of the building.

11

Under the Trees at Lincoln Center
with Elliod and Dan

In the shadow of Lincoln Center, a collection of white cube-shaped build-ings home to some of New York's most prized performing arts orga-nizations, Dan and Elliod sit under a canopy of trees just off the side of the Center's central plaza. Their seemingly vague instructions that I meet them "under the trees at Lincoln Center" prove blatantly obvious upon arrival here at one of the city's most iconic structures. The vivid oasis of greenery stands in stark contrast to the plaza's monochromatic, concrete-tiled pavement.

As I move through the courtyard and approach the pair, Dan and Elliod recline amid a smattering of other shade-seekers in two of the black modern circular chairs dotted beneath the arbor. Their bodies firmly sunken into their respective chairs, it appears that they have already been here for a while and are unlikely to have any pressing plans to leave. The shadow of the tree branches overhead provides relief from the ever-warm-ing afternoon sun, a respite especially desired by Dan and Elliod, who will spend the rest of the summer seeking daily refuge from the heat. Dragging an empty chair beside the two that Dan and Elliod have already claimed, I sit down and start to take stock of this world they have carved out for themselves.

Elliod instantly takes the lead in the conversation and explains what they did before arriving to this (often visited) spot. Playing with her blonde hair as she speaks, she explains that they had spent the morning at the LGBTQ homeless youth center where they are both members of the agency's daytime services drop-in center. Elliod also lives in a transitional apartment administered by this agency. Dan stays at a shelter run by a different group—the same shelter where la Princess is staying. Both housing agencies require Dan and Elliod to be out of the living space for from 8 a.m. to 8 p.m.

Speaking rapidly, Elliod discusses how she attended her housing center's trans group that morning; the group focuses on training young people to be advocates for trans rights and provides job training for its members. Mentioning she had recently taken a job-readiness credentials program, Elliod shares, "I passed it with flying colors. I was pretty proud of myself." She goes on to explain how she will attend the Trans Day of Action tomorrow with this group, and there is more than a bit of pride in her voice when she shares that she has been asked to speak on the group's behalf. Her posture straightens just a bit as she talks, her body seemingly buoyed by being selected to represent the group at tomorrow's event.

Hearing about his friend's plans, Dan breaks into Elliod's story to ask, "Can I go, too?" His head has turned in her direction, and his voice has slightly risen in volume, a small but noticeable departure from his usual flat, monotone affect. This change in tone signals a concern. He seems to be worried that his friend has made plans tomorrow without his knowing, plans that might not involve him. Elliod assures Dan that he is welcome to come. "Yeah, it's for allies, too. So we can go together." Dan settles back into his chair, relieved to hear the news.

"It's actually been a really good day," Elliod continues after a short lull in conversation. She goes on to share how, earlier today, she had been talking to a friend who was distraught over the wait for an HIV-test result, growing ever more sure it would come back positive. Elliod had stayed by his side for the next while as the friend talked about his worries. She had flagged a staff member at the center, and together they tried to calm his nerves and assure him that, regardless of the result, he would not be in danger of losing friends or the support he had at the center. "I felt that I could be a resource for him, and it proved to me that I should be the youth advocate, that I'm going to do well," she says, speaking a bit more quickly than before. Seemingly making herself happy by retelling the story, Elliod relays her actions earlier today with a firm sense of accomplishment, excited that she has done well by her friend and eager to share the story to her current audience of two.

Her words trail off as she realizes she has reached the story's conclusion. Looking over to Dan, she sees that he has relaxed well into his chair. His head lies back, face up to the trees, and his feet are kicked up on another chair. A coy smile appears on Elliod's face as she turns to me and says, "I know you want to talk about what we usually do here, why this is the spot . . . [Dan] makes me take pictures of him from all sorts of crazy angles, from over there to in front of that statue to in the trees and by the fountain. He makes me get down and shoot from all sorts of angles." Speaking in an animated manner, Elliod points in all directions, moving her body up and down, mimicking the physical toil Dan puts her through to get that perfect shot. Despite her poking a little fun at her companion's exercises in photographic vanity, Elliod's efforts leave Dan unfazed. I turn to Dan and ask him what he does with the photos. He barely mumbles a demure, "I don't know . . ." when Elliod sweeps back in before he can finish.

"He takes dozens upon dozens of photos and then maybe uses two or three, edits them cute together, and puts them on Instagram, updates those Grindr pictures," Elliod adds with a smirk. She offers no indication of remorse about talking for her friend, especially now that he has not moved to interrupt her. Whether or not Dan likes her sharing this information, his lack of reaction seems to indicate that Elliod is not misinterpreting any of the facts.

A moment of silence passes, and the wind sighs through the branches overhead. Elliod continues, this time more reflectively and, perhaps, attempting to assure her friend that she is just giving him a hard time. "I think it's important for a lot of the LGBT community now, like updating pictures and stuff, because I feel like they kinda have the mentality that you're selling yourself. . . . You need to have good pictures, you need to be, like, look neat and cute. You'll be more accepted if you are." After I prompt Dan by asking if he agrees with his friend, he adds that he likes when people like his posts and comment that he looks handsome. He then adds that he does not feel the need to post all the time, even though Elliod's description of his photo shoots make it seem as though he does. Perhaps he wants to distinguish that just because he *does* post a lot, it does not mean that he *needs* to do so.

Dan reclines in the shade, and I ponder his explanation of his social media habits. It is hard for me to follow as the sentences coming out of his mouth seem to lack punctuation. He is speaking in a low and quiet tone, more so than usual, and seems to be sinking farther down into his chair as the time passes. Worrying that the recorder will not pick up his comments, I ask him if he can speak a little louder. He acquiesces by sitting up a little straighter in his chair, but does not really raise his voice when he continues to speak. I wonder whether he's not interested in answering my questions or perhaps is just high from their daily self-pre-scribed dose of marijuana.

A few weeks earlier, Dan and Elliod explained during their first go-along how using marijuana helps combat the anxiety of occupying the streets for hours and hours each day. "When I'm not high, I'm always thinking about problems," Dan explained, adding that being high enabled him to focus instead on finding ways to solve the problems he faced. Elliod confessed that being high reduced her anxiety about passing as female while walking through the city, saying, "It makes it easier to walk the streets and not worry."

These previous confessions provide context for Dan's present mellow affect and slurred speech. Elliod's tendency to talk over, for, and about Dan seems to be an integral part of their modus operandi; their symbiosis includes her being his mouthpiece and his providing the companionship so that she does not have to face the streets alone. How they came to be involved in the study echoes this arrangement, as it was Dan whom I had initially recruited to be part of the project. At that first go-along, he showed up with Elliod in tow, and she proceeded to provide most of the commentary during the conversation. Afterward, she consented to be an official part of the study.

Continuing with today's conversation about their social media use, Elliod takes over for Dan and explains how she posts much less frequently, at least in contrast to her companion. "I think for me it's a lot different because going through a transition, doing it over social media can be kinda hectic. And then moving around so often, sometimes [social media] is my only way of keeping in contact with people I used to know." Elliod explains that maintaining an online presence can be very different for her because of both her gender transition and her frequent transitions in terms of location. She left home as a teenager before starting her gender transition, so many of her family members and friends only get updates about her life through her online posts. "That's how my family found out, through Facebook," Elliod explains, " 'cause I never disclosed to them, I never had a coming out, I never felt the need to. They just saw on Face-book that I was dressing more feminine and my hair was growing out."

Like Elliod, Dan is also geographically separated from his family. He came to the United States from Latin America on his own when he was eighteen. In our previous conversations, Dan shared very few details about the circumstances of how he got to New York and, furthermore, asked that I not write any of them down. Since they both came to New York from different places by themselves, their bond has proven to be a key part of how they have learned to navigate the city together. Their partnership has quickly grown into kinship.

During their previous go-along at Washington Square Park, the pair shared the simple origin of their friendship. They met at the LGBTQ youth housing agency, where they became fast friends. Elliod explained how one day, while they were seated next to each other, Dan just gave her a bottle of water without any prompting. "From there we just became friends, and we see each other every day now." This simple gesture of generosity was the catalyst for a fast friendship that then grew to become a consistent source of companionship. Elliod explained how Dan helped her get to know how to move around New York, even though he had only arrived in the city a few months before her. Sitting on a shaded bench near the park's famous arch, I was struck by their connection, by the ways they spoke for and with each other, by the ways they seemed like an inseparable unit. "We are family," Dan had said during the earlier go-along; Elliod smiled and added, "I feel the same way." Although I didn't know for sure, sensing the weight of this admission between the two of them felt as though it just might have been the first time they verbalized how much they meant to each other.

That conversation echoes in my mind as I sit with Dan and Elliod today, watching them tease each other about their social media habits—well, watching Elliod poke fun at Dan while Dan absorbs his friend's playful ribbing. Since Elliod mentions Dan's using the photos she takes of him for Grindr, I ask him what he thinks about the app. "I'm not on there all the time. But when I don't have nothing to do, I'll go in and check messages," he explains in his low tone before cracking a slight smile and adding, "And to see if there are cute guys . . . But I'm not on there all the time."

I notice a bit of defensiveness in the final part Dan's explanation, that he doesn't want me to think he's always just looking to hook up. Lest he think I'm judging him, I comment how some people use Grindr to pass the time without the intention of actually having sex, but he quickly denies doing that. The speed of his response makes me worry that my line of questioning is starting to impede rather than provide space for conversation. But then Elliod interjects, saying to Dan, "But you do use Grindr to pass time; you just said you go on when you have nothing to do." Following Elliod's comment, Dan admits to being confused by my question, though I'm not sure whether I asked it in a confusing way or whether he is perhaps too high to follow my line of inquiry. Or perhaps he is feeling self-conscious about talking about sex with another gay man.

I ask Dan whether the questions are getting too personal, but he assures me he doesn't care, before succumbing to a slight case of the giggles. I forge on, wanting to get a sense of whether Dan uses Grindr as a mechanism to help him get off the street during these long days of being out and about. I ask, "I know you have to be outside all day, right? And if you go to hook up with someone and then get to be inside for fifteen minutes . . . half an hour . . . however long it takes . . ." Before I can finish my question, Elliod sweeps in, half-speaking, half-laughing. "I really wanna tell [Sam] what happened yesterday, but it's your thing to share." Not surprisingly, Dan consents, and Elliod proceeds to share that yesterday while they were hanging out Dan turned to her and said, "I'm going to fuck, I'll be back in thirty to forty minutes." I ask how long he was gone, and Elliod confirms, "Literally thirty minutes."

"Sometimes that's all you need," I comment playfully, which makes Elliod laugh. Dan heartily voices his agreement: "I know!" As the pair's laughter subsides, I reflect on the power of the photo shoots. They seem to be an attempt to catch those moments when Dan feels good and feels that he looks good, using the endless supply of dramatic New York City backgrounds to add extra glamour and edge to the portraits he com- poses—with Elliod's assistance, of course! Through the process of curating his online photographic presence, he works to create and maintain images of himself that minimize any potential stigma about his present housing situation, the thinking being that the production of such images might serve to shift social gazes away from Dan's housing insecurity.

With such shifts, Dan's photographic maneuverings become some- thing other than acts of defiance or attempts to undermine cultural norms. Along these lines, Irit Rogoff offers a provocation to see attempts at "look- ing away [to] be understood not necessarily as an act of resistance to, but rather as an alternative form of taking part in culture."[1] Instead of framing Dan's actions as bold attempts at survival amid the cultural landscape, we can view them as ways of participating in such environments, denuded of negative assumptions. By compelling social gazes to turn away from the burdening normative expectations of what youth experiencing homeless- ness are assumed to look like, Dan puts forward his own self-produced representation of himself.

The photo shoots, and the resulting photos, provide Dan with the opportunity to go into someone else's house for a midday hookup, which allows for a brief reprieve from the elements and his daily wanderings through the city. Having desirable images of himself for his Grindr profile enables Dan to have interactions with men on the app, which potentially lead to Dan being invited into their homes. Beyond the sexual gratification, these invitations provide Dan with a chance to get off the streets. They offer a pause from extreme temperatures or precipitation, a chance to use a nonpublic restroom or take a shower, or just the opportunity to relax and even get some sleep on a bed that is likely to be more comfortable than the foldable cot he sleeps on every night at the shelter. The photo shoots prove to be a critical feature of Dan's experiences moving about the city. The photos literally help open doors for him; they shift the architecture of the city to his advantage. This photographic maneuvering is a result of Dan's savvy knowledge of ways to inhabit and move through the city while strategically avoiding gazes that constitute him as "homeless." It also demonstrates the sophisticated ways queer, non-binary, and trans youth use visual images differently than the normative constructions often traditionally associated with selfies and youth culture.[2] In learning to navigate both public and online spaces, Dan is able to carve out opportunities for himself while being transitionally housed.

"I don't really like hooking up or anything," Elliod says, before sheepishly conceding, "but I am on Grindr kinda for that reason. But I want to date someone; I want a real relationship." Her concession here contrasts with her earlier admission of identifying as demisexual—someone who prefers to have an intimate connection with another person prior to sexual contact. However, she explains that the circumstances of her life justify her desires, even if they sit in tension with other parts of her identity. She continues by explaining, "I think that's a little bit of the codependence I've learned from my family, a little bit of need of validation in my transition, a little bit of the hormones, and a little bit being homeless." Struck by her list of reasons for wanting (or needing) the comfort and relief of human contact and sexual gratification, I sense that she holds shame for admitting to wanting to have casual sex. In an attempt to assuage some of that feeling, I ask whether Elliod (and Dan, by proxy) feels that she can concurrently seek hookups and long-term dating opportunities, explaining that I often hear my friends struggle with the same dilemma—that if they put it out there that they are seeking casual sex, people will automatically assume they are not the dating type.

In response, Elliod shares that she struggles with what information to put in the text section of her Grindr profile. "My profile, usually, when I write it from my perspective . . . I'm like, 'I'm demisexual, I'm looking for something real and genuine.' But when I talk to the professionals over here," she says, gesturing to Dan with a grin, "and they're like, 'No, no, no, no. You need to just be open ended, ask them questions, don't say too much, what happens happens, and be okay with it.'" Although she took the advice and wrote her profile to be more vague as to what she was looking for, Elliod shares that even when she does go for a hookup, she only does so with men whom she could envision dating—even if she knows the encounter will only be a one-off. "Because that's what those apps are really geared toward in the end," she concludes.

Dan chimes in, "I honestly don't think I will get a boyfriend [off Grindr]. . . . If I meet a guy outside or at a bar, that's different. But if we start talking on Grindr, I'm not interested in [dating]." As he explains, it seems as though he sees Grindr as a somewhat tainted space, even if it is one that he himself frequents. According to Dan, any interaction with another guy that starts on the app is tinged by the specter of sex and cannot go anywhere past the resultant sexual encounter. Interested to hear him speak more about why he draws this distinction, I ask him why he thinks that a hookup cannot lead to anything more, or why he does not see Grindr (or other apps) as a space to meet guys for nonsexual encounters. After thinking for a moment, Dan replies emphatically, "Because he is looking for sex. Everyone there is looking for sex."

I want to ask more, but I start to wonder whether my line of inquiry is an attempt to poke holes in Dan's thinking rather than an opportunity to better understand Dan's thought processes. In truth, I sympathize with what Dan is saying. Throughout my own dating and sex life, I often struggle with whether it is possible to put myself out there as someone who wants to both hookup and date, while trying to resist heteronormative approaches to finding love and getting off. Seeing similar sentiments in Dan's explanations of the ways he uses Grindr, I sense that my questions are trying to offer a type of advice or to get him to be easier on himself. Before I can ask another question, however, my phone rings.

I look to see that it is Brian, with whom I was supposed to meet for a go-along earlier in the day. I apologize to Dan and Elliod and answer the call. Brian says he is at the Metropolitan Museum of Art, where I had been a few hours ago, waiting for him for over an hour. "I'm sorry, Brian, I thought we were meeting at 11:30 . . . Yeah, it looks like we missed each other," I say. Earlier today, while waiting for Brian on the front steps of the Met, I worried that perhaps he was there, hidden amid the crowd. I texted him to no avail. A few minutes later, as I wandered through the museum's massive lobby, I had a hunch I was being stood up. My thoughts went back to our go-along at the computer lab, when I had gotten the sense that, despite his consenting to participate, Brian was still uneasy about being interviewed. On the phone now, I tell Brian that I will see him at HMI later today, and he apologizes again before we hang up. After ending the call, I am left with an uneasy feeling, unsure whether today's missed go-along was just a scheduling mishap or was indicative of something more.

Turning my attention back to Dan and Elliod, I realize that my phone call had gone on long enough that they have moved the dialogue onto another topic, which they are discussing between themselves. I ask what they are planning to do before HMI opens later in the afternoon. Dan says he wants to take a few more pictures before they leave. Elliod rolls her eyes in response before agreeing to do so. As Elliod starts talking more about the photo shoots, Dan remains seated beside her in silence, only engaging in the conversation when Elliod or I ask him a direct question.

Their dynamic becomes more and more apparent. Elliod does the talking, and Dan provides the company. There is great value to the experience of being together as they find ways to take up time between the opening and closing hours of the various agencies they visit on any given day. After giving her friend another bit of grief about the photos, Elliod notes the importance of having Dan in her daily life: "When I'm by myself, I'm a lot more anxious; I'm a lot more antsy. I don't like having the body language of someone who is timid or nervous because then you are a lot more likely to be victimized or, you know, actually have someone come up and fuck with you because you look like you're *fuckwithable*. But when I'm with my friends, I feel a lot more confident, and I feel capable of saying what I want to people who walk by or glance by." Dan nods slowly from his chair in tacit agreement, with each passing moment seemingly ever more content with Elliod being his vocal representative.

While their current housing situations have the pair sleeping in different boroughs, over an hour-long train ride apart, they always find each other. Their daily meetup spot, either here or at a variety of other places they frequent, is often intuited by their memorizing the schedules of various agencies they access, based on what groups are running or which centers are open on certain days. Given that they don't always have cell phone or Wi-Fi access, knowing these routines becomes important to ensuring that they can connect. This spot under the trees at Lincoln

Center is, by their admission, one of their favorites. Well protected from the elements, away from major streets, and cut off from the sizzling concrete jungle beyond the shade of the trees, Elliod and Dan remain seated side by side, treasuring their cool refuge from the heat as the summer sun gets into gear in the sky above.

12

Meeting Axel's Posse

As Axel and I step into the Nintendo store in Rockefeller Center, the blaring Mario Brothers video game theme music funneling through the sound system makes it feel as though we have stepped into another dimension. The music so dominates the space that it seems I might need to leap over a piranha plant jutting up from the floor at any minute or look up for a coin block overhead. Axel and I have entered a video gamer's paradise.

As soon as he is through the door, Axel is in awe. Although he has been to this store many times, it is as if he is seeing the Holy Grail for the first time. He inhales slowly, and his eyes widen through his thin-framed glasses as he scans the array of figurines, stuffed dolls, and various video game–related paraphernalia with great enthusiasm. "Oh my god, that's Zelda's sword! It's gorgeous," he exclaims with wonder before turning to the next display. As we make our way through the store's ground level, each new character or object Axel sees is met with either an "Ooooooh" or an "Oh my god!" Axel reacts to each new sighting with an equal level of excitement.

"They have sweaters now. How cool. This is all new!" He holds the brightly colored garment up to his body; the sweater contrasts with his standard outfit of jeans and a gray T-shirt. The displays contain characters from various video games, comic books, and television franchises. Approaching each one, Axel identifies the character by name *and* by the series it is in. He also knows each story in intricate detail. At times, he is moving so fast that it is hard for me to follow him, especially with my limited knowledge of and experience with video games, comic books, and the like.

"You don't know *any* of these?" Axel asks me, gesturing with his hand over a shelf lined with hundreds of figurines. I reply, "Do I know any of these? I know . . . ," stalling as my eyes scan the shelves full of characters until I finally recognize one: "Yoshi. I know Yoshi." "That's a good one," Axel says, but his body is already in motion, yearning for the next set of products.

I catch up with Axel as he reaches for a Zelda backpack and with a smile takes it off the hook on the wall. Looking at it in his hands with admiration, he inspects the price tag. "How much is it? . . . Thirty dollars . . . Yeah, I don't have that much money," he says in a matter-of-fact tone, while running a hand through his dark curly hair. He does not seem surprised that the item is out of his price range. There is just a tinge of sadness in his voice, however, perhaps signaling that even though he knew it was going to be beyond his budget, there was a small part of him that had hoped he might be wrong.

After making a loop around the ground floor, Axel suggests we go upstairs. I ask him what is up there. With a growing smile, he responds, "Pokémon." His one-word response to my inquiry implies that this single word is enough of a description; from the power of this word alone, I should know what awaits us at the top of the stairs. However, video game neophyte that I am, I do not.

The arcade-themed music happens to crescendo as Axel leads the way up the stark white staircase, imbuing our ascent with a bit of dramatic flair. Half of the second floor of the store filled is with similar display shelves of more and more characters. The other half is lined with several large TVs, each with customers playing different video games. There are also two wall-sized screens where customers are playing video games with nearly life-size images.

Axel starts his exploration of the second floor in the displays. He reaches the Pokémon area and swiftly moves through, remarking with wonder as he sees each of the many characters from this series. Watching him say the names of character after character with a succinct description of their powers and backstories, I ask whether he would be able to recognize every character on display in the store. "Yes, I would," he says without hesitation, not looking up from the plush toy in his hand that he is currently inspecting.

"You know [what video game or series] everything is from?" I ask again, gesturing toward the rows and rows of products. "Yup," he repeats, before seeing another new character and exclaiming with awe, "Oooh, you gotta be kidding me!" A pattern repeats for the next few minutes: Axel sees a new character; he reacts with great emotion; I ask who it is; he explains in great detail who it is and where it is from; he looks at the price of the item (figure, plush toy, garment with character graphics on it, etc.); he laments because it is too expensive; he then moves on to the next item; the cycle begins anew. Although Axel wanted to come to this store for his go-along because he realized he had not visited in a while, it has become evident that perhaps his visits here are not for shopping purposes.

In just these first minutes of walking through the Nintendo store with Axel, it is clear that he has a particular relationship with the myriad of characters he encounters on the various shelves. His vast knowledge of their stories is only heightened by the contrast to my even more vast lack of familiarity with anything more specific than Mario, Luigi, Yoshi, and Princess Peach. He seems slightly befuddled when I admit my ignorance of many of the video games and comic book series he treasures, but my lack of familiarity is not enough to distract him from the series of joyful reunions he seems to be having each time he spots a new character.

I intuit from Axel's elated reaction upon seeing various figurines that they mean something more to him than just a creative escape; these fictional characters are of as much importance to Axel as the living people he knows and with whom he interacts. Axel's relationships to these characters and stories compel a conceptualization of the "field site" as expanding beyond the physical world[1] to include how these seemingly virtual interactions affect Axel's understanding of himself in relation to the worlds through which he moves. He admits that he has come to know these characters through seeing them in video games and television series, but being able to see these characters in the flesh, being able to hold them and pick them up in his hands, feels like a reunion of sorts. Physical connection to the characters appears to be something he craves and needs, dispelling the assumed binary between virtual worlds and the supposed real world.[2]

Axel's experiences with these characters prompt me to consider different ways of thinking about how he experiences the social world. It would be easy through certain lenses to paint Axel's fawning over video game characters as juvenile and immature, to assume that as a nineteen-year-old he should be investing his time in other pursuits. However, such senses of experience, to draw on Maria Lugones, "constrain, erase, or deem aberrant experience that has within it significant insights into non-imperialistic understanding between people."[3] For Axel, as a queer

Latinx young man, these characters provide connections that are missing from his life, given the ways he is disconnected from traditional social networks. His queered orientation to seemingly "fantastical" characters reflects, to borrow from Jorge Esteban Muñoz, "anticipatory illumination of certain objects [as] a kind of potentiality that is open, indeterminate, like the affective contours of hope itself."[4] They help Axel make sense of how he positions himself amid the normative racialized and sexual currents of the world that say he should be otherwise.

Axel's meandering path through the store leaves him staring up at the giant screen, watching a projected human-sized Mario run and jump across the wall under the direction of a young man with the controller halfway across the room. As luck would have it, just a few seconds later the young man loses the game and puts down the controller. Spotting his opening, Axel says to me excitedly, "C'mon!" and races to the Wii U game console. He picks up the controller and starts a round of the game *Mario Maker*. Less than ten seconds into his turn, he runs Mario off a cliff to the sounds of the recognizable Mario Brothers "end of turn" music. I remember the riff from playing on my friend's Super Nintendo back in middle school.

Axel offers me the controller to take a turn, but I tell him to have another go. He starts a new round. After collecting a few gold coins, however, Mario meets his demise again just seconds later. I am a little surprised. Given the in-depth knowledge Axel has been exhibiting and his extreme enthusiasm about being here, I figured he must also be good at playing the video games. Listening to him talk, I have been imaging him in his room growing up, reading these comics, watching these shows on TV, *and* playing these video games.

"Okay, you try," he says, handing me the controller, telling me which buttons to press for jumping and the other actions without my asking for help. I start my round, and Mario begins running across the screen. About thirty seconds into my turn, I have already gone further than both of Axel's first two attempts combined. Trying to downplay how far I've gotten, I say, "I'm really bad at video games." My worry that Axel might be embarrassed by my showing him up at his own game is immediately dispelled, however, as I catch a quick glimpse him standing beside me, staring up at the screen.

Axel cheers, "All right, Mister Awesome!" He is enthusiastically praising my skills as he mimics Mario's movements with his body as if to help move our red-capped hero along telepathically with his motions.

Axel is just as happy as he's been the entire time we've been in the store, providing color commentary as I navigate Mario through the level. "Oh, snap!" . . . "Go to the door" . . . "Yoshi, no! Yoshiiiii" . . ." Dang it!" After a few minutes, Mario's life is cut short again, this time at my hands.

Putting down the controller, we walk past a museum-like display case, chronicling the history of the handheld Game Boy console. Axel comments, "It's like the whole evolution! It's incredible." Through the glass, we point out the versions we each used to have when we were younger. Mine was one of the original versions with the two-toned green-and-black pixelated screen (on which I only remember playing a tennis game), while he had the more advanced Game Boy Color, a version of the game system that featured a colored screen. Making our way back down the stairs, Axel is diverted from the exit by a display he had not seen during our first lap. "Oh, I'm amazed they have my *favorite* character," he says. This is a sentiment he has expressed more than a few times already on our visit to the store. He is soon admiring another figurine, the Mad Hatter (as portrayed by Johnny Depp in the live-action *Alice in Wonderland* movie).

A Nintendo store employee sees Axel holding the figurine with admiration and asks whether we need any help. "I'm good," he replies with a smile before returning the Mad Hatter to the shelf and turning to head toward the door. I ask if he's going to get anything. "No, I don't have any money. I just came to look," he replies as he starts to move to the exit. Two steps later, however, he starts to peruse another display. Although he has intimated twice already that he is ready to leave, he seems to be doing everything he can to stay in the store. Stopping at the last display before the door, Axel explains his family's thoughts about his relationship to the video game and comic book worlds: "This makes me totally different [from them]. They are all into sports and junk and stuff like that." He adds that he attributes his love of these characters to the influence of a few friends and especially one of his cousins, who first introduced him to these genres.

As Axel speaks about his family, we finally make it to the door and move out onto the sidewalk. There is a bit of a drop in his affect as he starts to talk about his family. The sensation is only intensified by the diminishing of the bright and peppy video game soundtrack as wander away from the store and continue down 48th Street. This is a rare moment when the streetscape sounds of New York City seem calm and tranquil in comparison to the frenetic energy and commotion inside the Nintendo store.

A few steps later, Axel's head darts over his shoulder as he gasps, audibly, from out of nowhere. Relaxing a fraction of second later, he explains, "Oh, I thought I saw my mother" and continues walking, realizing he was mistaken. There was no way she would be here in Manhattan when she lives and works in the Bronx. As we walk, I think about Axel's artwork—he is a very skilled sketch artist. We first met one day at HMI when I was passing through the art room and saw him hard at work, drawing one his favorite characters, who I now know to be from the Pokémon franchise. The precision and talent in his artwork parallel how he expresses his deep-seated knowledge about these characters through his words and through his hands.

I ask about his relationship with his mother and how she views his love of the creative aspects of the fantasy world, including his own artwork. "[My mom] thinks it's a waste of my talent. And I'm like, '*Mother*, it's what I love.' And she just shuts right up." I've heard Axel speak to his mother on the phone before, switching between Spanish and English. Despite his frustrations with her, throughout previous go-alongs he frequently checked in with her via phone and text to keep her apprised of his whereabouts. Even though he has the freedom to move about the city to travel to school and HMI, I sense that he always feels as though his mother is watching.

We reach the end of the block and wait for the light at 6th Avenue to turn green. Just as Axel seems to adjust to the drop in energy after leaving the Nintendo store, he starts to restore his mood. "There's an anime store just around the corner. Wanna go?" he asks, though the question mark is really only a formality. I readily agree, and Axel quickly turns toward his destination, his excitement leading his body through the crowded sidewalk.

John's Grandmother Has Some Questions

Three generations of Black women unload a carful of shopping bags printed with the labels of various merchants. They take turns reaching into the car's trunk or through one of the open doors to grab part of the day's shopping haul. Carrying whole armloads of food and household goods, the women move in rotation up the short driveway into their crisply painted, two-story home. Their house is one in a row of proudly manicured detached homes along a tree-lined block in East Flatbush, Brooklyn.

Half a block down, I stand on the sidewalk, trying to look inconspicuous while waiting for John to emerge from their grandmother's house. From three or four houses away, I try to nod hello politely when I sense that one of the women is looking my way, but it isn't clear that she can see my gesture from this distance. I know from walking along this street on John's previous go-along that this neighborhood is made up of a majority of Black and Afro-Caribbean residents; further, the blocks upon blocks of detached single-family homes also signal that this as a decidedly middle-class enclave.[1] As John led the way home a few weeks earlier, they commented how this neighborhood's racial makeup was drastically different from where they previously lived in Florida. "I was used to like ninety-eight percent Caucasian white people," they explained. "I came here and was so astounded to see all this different type . . . of diversity. It was crazy!"

I noted on that first go-along how various streets were proudly marked with banners, indicating several different neighborhood associations proclaiming these streets to be of and for the residents. On that walk, seeing the neighborhood's nicely manicured lawns and well-kept homes led me to assume that this area's residents were largely homeowners. In contrast to other majority-Black neighborhoods throughout the city, where neighborhoods have been claimed by various communities of color by virtue of their long-standing residence, this neighborhood seems to bolster their claim to this place with residence *and* property ownership, an important distinction that counters dominant stereotypes about the precarious economic and tenancy situations of many predominately Black and Latinx neighborhoods throughout New York. On that first go-along, John mentioned that their grandfather, a West Indian immigrant whom they had never met, had built the family house himself and that John's grandmother had lived in it ever since. Even though John had only lived with their grandmother in this house for a short while, they mentioned knowing a few of the neighbors who were longtime friends of their grandparents.

Now, on my second trip to this neighborhood, I recognize that my whiteness not only stands out visually but could also be considered a potential threat to the Black homeownership of this community,[2] that I might just be another white person here to gentrify the neighborhood. Knowing that John's grandmother is not keen on her grandchild being out of the house at all (not to mention her disapproval of John's gender and sexual fluidity), I decide it is best not to wait directly in front of John's house lest their grandmother peek out the window.

Five minutes after texting John about my arrival, they come bounding down the front steps of the house to the sidewalk and turn to walk toward me. Clipping the microphone onto their lapel, John leads us down the sidewalk in the direction of bustling Flatbush Avenue and away from the women unloading the car. With the neighbor women behind us, it is impossible to gauge their reaction to the sight of a white man walking away with John, whom I assume they might know as their neighbor's eighteen-year-old granddaughter.

We walk down the street a few blocks, and I check in to confirm that they are going by "John" today. On days when John feels more feminine, they go by a different name and use she/her pronouns. Their style of dress tends to remain consistent; they usually don a pair of jeans and hoodie, so there is little visual evidence as to how their gender is showing up each day. John confirms I should use *they*, and explains we are going to walk to the hospital where they have an appointment with their psychiatrist. I tell them that this is going to be the very last go-along of the entire study.

They start to apologize that they do not have time to do more go-alongs, referring to a few previously planned go-alongs that they had to cancel. Just then, their phone rings. "Oh, sorry, it's Grandma." They pick up the call with a tinge of exasperation upon greeting their guardian to whom they just bid farewell moments earlier.

"Whaaa? . . . No, I'm fine," they retort into their cell phone. We walk in silence, John listening to their grandmother. I notice the sound of a car's tires screeching lightly along the pavement as it turns a corner around us while we wait to cross the street.

Still on the phone, John starts to speak again, "No, it's a guy from HMI. He's doing an essay—[*whispering*] I already told you about this. He's doing like a dissertation for college. [*Silence as they listen to Grandma*] He's basically just following me and seeing what I do each day . . . or some days, anyway. [*Silence as they listen to Grandma*] Well, today's our last day, so—[*silence as they listen to Grandma*] I met him outside, so we are on our way to the hospital."

After a few more rounds of questioning, the inquisition seems to be waning. John's tone shifts to indicate a bit of relief, and they offer a few more "yeahs" into the telephone before telling their grandma they will see her when they get home. "Sorry," John says to me. "I guess I was a little too cryptic when I told her there was a guy outside."

Hearing John's description of the project—"He's just following me around"—causes a pang of dread in my chest. On the very last day of my project, whatever sense of comfort or ease I have developed as a researcher, whatever insight I have gained about what it means to move with these youth from the city, is cast aside in this moment. John's description is clarifying in that regardless of whatever reflexive positioning I have done to ensure this project's ethicality and no matter how many levels of permission I have secured to get this project off the ground—approval from the ethics board; permission from HMI; John's own consent to participate—at the end of the day I am still a grown white man following this young genderfluid person of color around the city.

In contrast to my fearful reaction, however, John's explanation to their grandmother about the study suggests that they do not see any problem with their participation in the go-alongs—or with their moving through the city with a man they only know through their involvement at HMI. John seems to be stating that as an eighteen-year-old person, they should have the autonomy to do what they want, including the right to tell their grandma they are meeting a man outside the house just so he can follow them around. John's admission that they may have been intentionally cryptic with their explanation, however, suggests that perhaps giving their grandmother a bit more information about my presence could have saved them the hassle of dealing with her panicked phone call.

About fifteen minutes later, after John and I are just getting into a conversation about the dynamics of their gender identity, Grandma calls again. John picks up and starts to answer another series of (grand)parental questions. Each response is succinct and firm, but with just enough of a frustrated tone in John's voice to ensure that their objection to this rapid-fire inquiry is audible. After a bit of back-and-forth, John lowers the phone, explaining with a bit of exasperation, before handing me the phone, "I guess she wants to make sure you're not a serial killer by talking to her . . . or something."

For the sake of quickly alleviating Grandma's concerns, I take the phone, attempting to swallow my apprehension. I cover the speaker with my hand and confirm with John that I should use their government name and female pronouns when speaking with their Grandma. John quickly affirms that I should do so. Placing the phone to my ear, I greet the grandmother warmly and begin to field another round of questions, often having to repeat myself because we are standing on a very noisy street corner. John stands beside me, wincing periodically and seeming more and more embarrassed with each of my responses to their grandma's litany of questions. I try to assure her that I am working with HMI and that my study has the agency's full backing.

While she may not fully comprehend (or approve) that HMI serves LGBTQ youth, John's grandmother knows (and is happy) that John has a paid internship there. I know from previous conversations with John that their grandmother has been in regular communication with John's internship supervisor, so I make sure to mention to her that HMI staff members know about this project and of John's participation in it, hoping it will help her feel more comfortable with me by association. This strategy appears to be working, but she then inquires whether I have any sisters. I assure her that, as the elder brother to two sisters, I understand her wanting assurance that her grandchild is safe and sound. She seems appeased enough by my answer, and we hang up on a pleasant note.

I hand the phone back to John. As we continue our walk, John apologizes profusely for my having to do this, but my mind has already started to worry about whether their grandmother's concerns have been quelled. My consternation about the conversation with their grandmother makes me more and more tense as move down the same Brooklyn sidewalk John and I had traversed weeks before, this time in reverse. As we retrace our steps and I continue to worry about the call, it feels a bit as though the project is undoing itself, that I am moving back in time toward the start of the study.

Nearly thirty minutes later, we step into John's favorite calzone place because they have some time to kill before their appointment. The restaurant is near John's school, so they visit it frequently and have come to know one of the guys who work there. John orders a calzone right away after walking in, without even looking at the menu. Sitting down at a table, John pulls out their phone to respond to a text from their boyfriend. I join them a minute later after buying a ginger ale.

"I'm a little disappointed. I thought the guy I saw [behind the counter] was my guy, but it's not," John laments, looking up from their phone to gesture to the person behind the counter who took their order. Looking back to me, John asks if I watch *Game of Thrones*. We chat for a moment about our shared appreciation of the show. When it becomes clear that John has yet to see the most recent episode, I promise not to spoil anything. Noting the time, I tell John that I have to get going to head to HMI. I thank John for taking part in the study, telling them how much it means to me that they were so generous with their time. John apologizes for canceling some of our planned go-alongs and wishes they could have done more. I assure them the time they had to give was appreciated nevertheless.

John unclips the microphone from their collar and hands the recorder to me. I turn it off and pack it into my bag just as John's calzone arrives at the table. John looks up and smiles. It is their guy. He had been out of sight in the back kitchen when we first arrived. John thanks him, taking the tray from his hands and placing it on the table. The guy asks whether John wants a soda. John admits to only having enough money for the calzone. The guy smiles and turns away from the table before returning a moment later with a can of soda and a straw. He places both on the table and winks at John before disappearing back into the kitchen.

14

You Breaking Up with Me, Sam?

After leaving John at the calzone place, I arrive at HMI later that afternoon on what is my last scheduled day of volunteering. Now that my fieldwork has come to an end, I am due to leave New York in a couple of days. Today, I had set aside some time after my final go-along to bid farewell to youth and staff at HMI. My hope was to have a few final moments to say goodbye to both those youth who were in the study and those who were not.

As soon as I step off the elevator into the ever-frenetic lobby, however, I learn from the receptionist that John's grandmother has been repeatedly calling HMI, trying to reach John's internship supervisor to ask questions about me. As the supervisor is out sick, the calls have been bouncing around to a few other staff members. I spend the next few hours talking to staff and sending emails to ensure that John's supervisor and the program director know about the situation in case John's grandmother calls again after I leave HMI. It feels ironic that I must spend this very last day of research clearing up a situation that I had all along feared might arise. If this had happened in the first month or two of the study, it would have been one thing. But a day meant to for saying goodbye and reflecting on the study is instead consumed with efforts to ensure that I've covered all my tracks.

Even though the past months have involved considerable work and reflection on my part to let go of such preoccupations, I find all my worries about being a "good" researcher streaming back. To think, when I arrived at that last go-along with John just a few hours ago, I felt so good about the project. I was so proud that I was about to successfully complete fieldwork, so impassioned by all my conversations with the participants. Perhaps, I was also feeling a bit cocky that everything had gone off without a major hiccup.

Leaving HMI after programs have ended for the day and the youth have all left for the night, I feel considerably frantic. The smooth last day I envisioned did not come to fruition. Walking into the creaky elevator to leave HMI one last time, I feel that were wasn't sufficient time to bid farewell to the youth (both those in the study and other HMI members whom I had gotten to know through my volunteer work) or to thank the staff for their assistance with and support of the project over the past months.

As in most of the conversations that have taken place during the go-alongs, a train of thought or an impassioned confession could easily be interrupted by the sound of a passing car, the sight of a far-off building, the emergence of a long-repressed emotion, or countless other factors. At the start of each go-along, it was often unknown where the youth would end up by the conclusion of the session, emotionally or geographically. The study feels similarly interrupted. I have the feeling of being stranded in the middle of the city that I thought I knew so well. The research project, in all its facets, is left reverberating in, around, and through me—reverberations of the conversations with youth on park benches and in computer labs, of standing silently next to a participant as the train bursts into the station, of the canceled meetings and the meaningful reunions, of having questions posed to me by participants rather than answering the ones I posed to them, of thinking about how to move alongside them in respectful and meaningful ways as they navigate their everyday lives.

As the elevator descends to street level, a conversation with Scarlet from a few weeks earlier comes to mind. I had been asking her about scheduling our last go-along when I noticed she was wearing the shirt she bought during her previous interview at Burlington Coat Factory. The simplicity of the monochromatic button-up offered no indication of the strife that had gone into buying it or her long history of trying to find clothes from the men's department that fit her body. After I complimented her on the new look, she smiled, as if trying to hide her trademark rosy-red cheeks underneath her thick-rimmed glasses, and responded, "Thanks! I got it with my best friend!" We laughed, though her statement was perhaps both a joke and a not-so-subtle indication that our relationship meant something more to her than the normative, dispassionate researcher–subject relationship might normally allow. Her words signaled an awareness of social rules and her skillful tiptoeing around and through them. Her words highlighted an acknowledgment of her body as being a subject in this research project, and that she refused to let the flow of knowledge and information be a one-way street. Our conversation continued in a similar manner when I reminded Scarlet that the next go-along would probably be our last.

"Oh, you breaking up with me, Sam?" she guffawed with a purposeful exaggeration, perhaps an attempt to hide her true feelings. Perhaps the experience of the go-alongs had done something to her, taken her somewhere new, someplace she was just realizing as they were coming to an end.

"See, why you gotta go and be all dramatic?" I retorted, similarly doing the double work of matching her tone to show my willingness to meet her where she was while taking internal stock of how the go-alongs had moved and changed what I thought I knew about youth and what I thought this research project would produce. There is no ending to this research besides the one that presents itself, an ending filled with unanswered questions, canceled go-alongs, concerned grandmothers, and humorous verbal sparring that masks some deeper feelings.

The elevator reaches the ground floor and opens to the brightly colored mural painted on the foyer walls by HMI members of years past. Leaving the memory of Scarlet's laughter in the elevator, I take a few short steps through the foyer and push the glass door open onto the Greenwich Village sidewalk. My thoughts and preoccupations about the research project are instantly enfolded into the thick summer air and the crisscrossing flow of pedestrians. The last lingering worry from the phone call with John's grandmother works its way out of my mind and off my shoulders as my body is swept into the current of the city.

Coda

Landing at LaGuardia

There is a flight path frequently taken by planes on their way into landing at New York's LaGuardia Airport that provides a staggering aerial view of the city. As I look down from the window on the right side of aircraft, the tip of Manhattan appears as the plane starts to trace up the western edge of the island. As the plane races over the Hudson River at a deceivingly close height, the buildings are in such proximity it seems as if I could pick them up, hold them in my hand, and rearrange their placement at whim. The traffic along the West Side Highway is clear to the naked eye, and the bridges along the east side of the island seem superfluous from this perspective, as it appears as if one could step over the East River to Brooklyn and Queens with little effort.

From this window seat, the entire city is within reach; it can be appraised with one scanning glance. New York does not look scary or overwhelming or bustling. Rather, it appears calm, organized, and oddly tranquil. Droves of landmarks can be spotted as the plane zooms ahead, including those considered to be parts of "essential" New York—Times Square, Central Park, the Chrysler Building—and those that are essential parts of the city for the young people in the study. There is Union Square, where la Princess reflects on her morning, experiencing slight after transphobic slight at a series of back-to-back appointments at various government agencies. There is Lincoln Center, where Elliod and Dan rest, hidden below the trees alongside the Metropolitan Opera building after one of their frequent photo shoots where they produce photos to update their Facebook, Instagram, and Grindr profiles in hopes of presenting online images that counter dominant narratives about young people who are trans, queer, homeless, refugee, and so on. Further east, over one of the bridges, John sits in a Brooklyn pizza shop, enjoying their calzone and free bottle of soda, a gift from the guy behind the counter when John admits to not having enough money to buy it themself. After running the length of Manhattan, the plane takes a right over the Bronx to turn back toward its landing spot in Queens. With the expanded view provided by the plane's starboard-tilted rotation, the three group homes where Warby lived during the study's six-month span are somewhere below, spread out over the northernmost borough.

This elevated perspective of New York City, where its overwhelming street-level grandeur can still be felt though in a more contained and muted fashion, makes it seem as though getting to know the city is as easy as taking a once-around survey offered by this aeronautical experience. Despite the decreasing elevation, the city appears devoid of feeling through the cold plastic airplane window. From up here, there are no screeching subway cars that come rumbling into the station to interrupt Foxxy as they are explaining their fears of being in public as a non-binary person. It is not possible to witness the mental turmoil of Anna's inner monologue as she sits on one of her hour-long solitary train rides, wondering whether she will be able to make it to class *and* the grocery store, *and* still have time to help her younger sister with her homework before she heads to make her shift dancing at the club. Also lost are Scarlet's protests when her *abuelita* forces her to buy dress shirts from the "women's" section of Banana Republic in Jackson Heights in Queens, and Brian's quiet laughter as he watches clips of *Love & Hip Hop Atlanta* in the computer lab at his favorite public library near downtown Brooklyn. Once the plane touches down on the tarmac at LaGuardia, the energetic volume of the city ratchets all the way up as soon as the passengers deplane into the airport's overcrowded terminal. The moving pieces of the city, that only moments ago seemed like objects in a doll's house, are now obstacles and opportunities to move between and around and through and toward.

This process of descending into the city captures the core methodological frame of this project, a way to rethink common approaches to going along with young people. The shift from thirty thousand feet to street level brings along with it the need for adjustments of perception and sensation—namely, assessments that analyze how power is felt and experienced. From on high, the city appears calm and complete; all there is to see there can be accounted for from this specific perch. However, when the city is up close and personal, any single stretch of sidewalk abounds with sights, sounds, and smells to take in and process. Each block is as vast and grand as the city as a whole. In the midst of the concrete jungle, people bolt past one another before it is possible to fully assess the entirety of each person's dynamic wardrobe choices before the next person or the next intersection requires their attention.

Sidewalks, however, are not always about movement. They are not always transitory spaces, given that many New Yorkers occupy the sidewalk in a semipermanent fashion while others stream past them. The sidewalk, then, is a back-and-forth in directing and diverting attention, in movement and stillness, in going and staying. Immersing this research study in the city has forced me to shift the directions from which I view youths' movements through the city and to reconsider how my knowledge about them results from my viewing. It has forced an inclusion of youths' moments of stillness, of staying put, of not speaking, of passing time into an interview-based study about youth mobility.

Listening to Foxxy talk about the gender policing they experience while walking through the city takes on new meaning when the very bodies doing the policing are circling around them as they speak. While I stand beside them, I do my best to listen and still notice the reactions of passersby to Foxxy's body and gender presentation. It is not, however, that experiencing this event alongside Foxxy makes it more real because the experience is visible to the researcher's eye. Rather, the importance of moving, being, and going along with youth during these experiences is to consider the parts of these moments that might not be part of how the young people describe them—the quick back-and-forth scanning that Foxxy's eyes perform as their body moves down a sidewalk, the way their head jerks over their shoulder not because of a noise but because of a sensation that someone, somewhere, is staring at them, a feeling I also sense being next to Foxxy as my head makes similar movements along with theirs.

Such a moment involves grappling with ways to describe and represent these moments. "Because I felt it, too!" does not suffice as academic explanation of what is happening to youth, nor does it do justice to representing the intricate and sophisticated methods youth have developed in order to navigate intersecting forces through the city. Perhaps, as Maggie MacLure suggests, "We are obliged to acknowledge that data have their ways of making themselves intelligible to us."[1] Certain moments of "data" remain as imprints in my mind rather than as words recorded on a tape or an interview transcript. The emotional countertransference I experience in this moment moving alongside Foxxy is neither fact nor proof of any one thing. Being there alongside them in this moment prompts different questions, different avenues of thinking, different ways of understanding how Foxxy interacts with the social worlds around them.

The fluctuating perceptions of New York upon arriving in the city from on high, when buildings shift from looking tiny to looking bigger than life, parallel a shift in perception of young people from only ever looking at, being with, and talking to them in a singular manner or with a static framework. From a stratospheric perspective, youth appear as whole, as objects to be read and analyzed by the world around them. It is thought that they can be firmly located as being here or there, that they can be perceived easily as this or that, and that their actions can be decisively labeled as good or bad. However, being on sidewalks, subway platforms, and park benches beside the young people in this study enables me to consider diverging perspectives on what it means to experience the period of "youth." Such a positioning allows reflection on how, for example, riding the train for hours each day affects Anna's ability to talk about her daily routine; how the presence of street-involved New Yorkers sleeping on nearby park benches influences how la Princess mentally sketches out her future steps; how Axel's relationship with his family affects his ability to make the art he loves; or how the quiet buzzing of the library computer lab provides space for Brian to take a break from the ebbs and flows of the city.

The city, in general, provides fecund opportunities for shifting ways of thinking about youth. The fact that youth make their lives in every corner of the city counters the assumptions that youth possess a certain naïveté about social space and that the city is inherently dangerous and unknown, especially to its younger inhabitants. The city is often described as a place to go to "lose yourself," where youth can go to have unadulterated adventures in this city that survives without slumber. It is also thought to be a place where youth can escape to shed former personal baggage and embrace their supposedly truer selves. It is at the same time a place people seek out to safely express and present themselves and, as the largest urban metropolis in the US, a place often assumed to be full of crime and danger (no matter how much they have cleaned up Times Square).

New York City is simultaneously a place that people, often white, move away from when they want to have children *and* a home to the over one million children who are predominately of color, attending NYC public schools. Determining whether New York is suitable for youth, then, is solely based on the perspective from which one looks at it—from above or from the ground, from downtown or from uptown—and how one's own perspective of the city and its inhabitants is based on racialized, gendered, and classed experiences.

These perspectives, moreover, are created over time through the ways one comes to know (about) the city. The speed at which New York is thought to flow—that a New York minute is somehow less than sixty seconds—speaks, at the very least, to the sense that the city's residents project ownership of and knowledge about the city that enables them to navigate it at speeds that do not allow a second-guessing of where they are headed or how they are going to get there. From up high, it is not clear that a minute in New York is purportedly less than a minute elsewhere. On the ground, however, time in New York moves at various speeds, both upholding and dispelling the myth of time moving faster in the Big Apple. New York minutes could move faster for la Princess as she rides back and forth on the Staten Island Ferry to pass time on the days the social service agencies she frequents are closed, but they could also move more slowly for her in the fleeting time she has to get ready in the morning before having to set off from her shelter each day at 8 a.m. sharp. Time is perhaps moving simultaneously in diverging directions for Axel, who is not sure when he will work up the courage to talk to the boy he is crushing on, and for Scarlet, who is counting down the days until she is able to get out of the city to start her AmeriCorps placement.

To borrow from Elizabeth Freeman: such accounts of time can "elaborate ways of living aslant to dominant forces,"[2] ways in which youth experiences are too commonly cast aside as being unimportant but that can be vital indications of the ways in which youth envision their futures and the multidirectional paths they might take to get there.[3] It should not be forgotten that the seemingly calm, static New York that is visible from the landing route into LaGuardia can be experienced on the ground as well. There are pathways through the crowds, hidden corners of parks, and countless places throughout the city—obvious or not—that offer moments and spaces of refuge to some. Moreover, there are those for whom masses of people, boisterous noises, and frenetic public spaces *are* types of reflective sanctuaries, used to chart out future pathways through the city. Jam-packed parks on sunny afternoons, overflowing rush-hour subway cars, or other easily accessible spaces that are swarming with people can often offer a reprieve for young people who are under constant surveillance. There are times when it is possible—and arguably a necessary form of survival—to get lost in a crowd where the collective weight of surveillance is dispersed over myriad bodies to avoid its being focused on a single youth whose gender identity, housing situation, HIV status, race, or presentation makes such concentrated attention a source of danger. This purposeful accounting for differences in perspective, even when it explodes the assumption that social subjects—humans, cities, or otherwise—can ever been viewed as "whole," serves as a reminder that perspective is always coming from somewhere, from some specific angle, and through a certain filter. The view of New York City during the descent into LaGuardia is only accessible to those with the means to travel by air, those with the privilege to witness, firsthand, an aerial, panoramic view of the city.

The ability to see the entire city from up high, of being able to holistically read the city-as-text, harkens back to Michel de Certeau's description of Gotham from the 110th floor of one of the fallen towers, in which he comments that one's "body is no longer clasped by the streets that turn and return it according to an anonymous law; nor is it possessed, whether as player or played, by the rumble of so many differences and by the nervousness of New York traffic."[4] Access to this high vantage point, however, must be considered when researchers make observations about the city—or about the young people within it—and cannot leave behind their identities while doing the viewing. The knowledge gained from those who can access these locations to make such determinations results from having the privilege to be in those elevated places—both de Certeau from the observatory deck of that highest of buildings and myself from a descending airplane. Not every person has the ability to make such removed, detached assessments of the city and, in the case of this study, its youthful inhabitants. Moreover, there is the issue of how to avoid replicating research's colonial gaze when making said determinations.[5]

Such an understanding includes how youth are making sense of the city itself and, moreover, how society acknowledges that "the city" always already carries divergent and specific meanings to each youth, even when they point to the same exact piece of land and say, "*This* is New York." They may be motioning, generally, in the same direction and calling it the same thing, but that does not mean "New York" holds identical meanings for each person, nor are said meanings constituted in the same manner. As Colson Whitehead said, "You start building your private New York the first time you lay eyes on it. . . . Freeze it there: that instant is the first brick in your city."[6] Any given street, neighborhood, city, and so on is rife with contingent, conflicting histories and knowledges about whom each place is for, who has a right to be there, and who sets the rules that govern the area.[7] Even when a place is referred to with the same name by different people, the name is imbued with meanings that are not identical. Likewise, disciplinary knowledge about what, who, and where youth are assumed to be is used to point to an idealized image of the youth body[8] and communicate, "*This* is what a youth is," even if it is never entirely clear in what direction the pointing finger is aimed or to whose body the pointed finger is connected. Without specific attention paid to the normative power systems behind the pointing figure and the collective social attention that follows such an act of indication, the label "youth" often works to erase specific constructions of race, gender, sexuality, nationality, class, and ability.[9] Emplacing this study about youth within the ebbs and flows of New York City centralizes the concurrent constructions of and experiences with place and identity.[10]

This book takes seriously the perspectives that influence, assess, and shape experiences of young people in the city, making specific attempts to determine how said perspectives have led to and continue to promulgate assumptions about which experiences are good or bad, safe or unsafe, for or not for young people. Moreover, young people's views of the city are seen as leading to the creation of specific understandings of the city. A person's "thirty-thousand-foot view" of the city might have been achieved from atop a park bench, in the back of a subway car, in the middle of a throng of people, or on any given street corner. A person's "panoramic" understanding of the city does not always mean they have literally seen the city from above or that their journeys have taken them to every inch of the official city limits. In Whitehead's ode to his hometown, *The Colossus of New York,* he explains how a person's age of first contact with NYC influences how they build the city in their mind. Writing from the perspective of a child who first visits the city with their parents, he notes: "The only skyscrapers visible from your stroller were the legs of adults, but you got to know the ground pretty well and started to wonder why some sidewalks sparkle at certain angles, and others don't." In regard to his own experience, he explains: "I started building my New York on the uptown No. 1 train. My first city memory is of looking out a subway window as the train erupted from the tunnel on the way to 125th Street and palsied up onto the elevated tracks."[11] The experiences of young people in and with the city, then, are examined here in order to observe the specificity of those experiences rather than have them extrapolated in ways that view both youth and the city as static, preordained concepts controlled by the limitations of normative ways of looking at the social world.

While de Certeau suggests that "it is as though the practices of organizing a bustling city were characterized by their blindness,"[12] the methodological positioning of this study does not configure said "blindness" as something that is missing from the puzzle. Rather, there are always gaps in knowledge about youth and their experiences in the city. This does not mean that the inability to view the entire field of knowledge about youth, as a whole, is a limitation or an oversight. Instead, I acknowledge that attempts to see youth in their entirety—ascribing to the assumption that youth can ever be fully "known"—not only are impossible but amount to acts of violence that shave off important parts of youth and their experiences to make them visible within one (normative) viewing. As researchers, we must learn to resist the ways that our viewing of youth and their experiences as complete often collapse the specifics of their lives and lived experiences. Such a shift away from the temptation to always seek wholeness can lead to ways of knowing and thinking about youth that resist the disciplinary limitation of seeing "youth" as a cohesive, unitary category that is experienced in the same way by every person. Instead, young people can be seen as representing multifaceted experiences of age, race, gender, sexuality, nationality, and ability. Going along with the youth in this study, I hope, offers a way to reappraise not what youth are but what they have the potential to become.

Notes

Introduction

1. Margarethe Kusenbach, "Street Phenomenology: The Go-along as Ethnograhic Tool," *Ethnography* 4, no. 3 (2003): 455–85, https://doi.org/10.1177/146613810343007.

2. I use *cis* here tepidly and not because I claim to identify as such but because it is likely to be who or what I am assumed to be based on readings of my body and gender presentation. I share Finn Enke's concern that "cis" often "performs as the arbiter of real, true, or natural gender." I wish to avoid perpetuating such assumptions, but also want to elucidate how my body is perceived in general and during the go-alongs. Finn Enke, "The Education of Little Cis: Cisgender and the Discipline of Opposing Bodies," in *Transfeminist Perspectives in and beyond Transgender and Gender Studies*, ed. Finn Enke (Philadelphia: Temple University Press, 2012), 60–77.

3. Eric Rofes, "Bound and Gagged: Sexual Silences, Gender Conformity and the Gay Male Teacher," *Sexualities* 3, no. 4 (2000): 439–62, https://doi.org/10.1177/136346000003004005; Jonathan G. Silin, "Teaching as a Gay Man: Pedagogical Resistance or Public Spectacle?" *GLQ: A Journal of Lesbian and Gay Studies* 5, no. 1 (1999): 95–106.

4. Jules Gill-Peterson, "From Gender Critical to QAnon: Anti-Trans Politics and the Laundering of Conspiracy," *New Inquiry*, September 13, 2021.

5. David Stovall and Subini Annamma, "Using Critical Race Theory to Understand the Backlash to It," *Hechinger Report*, 2021, https://hechingerreport.org/opinion-using-critical-race-theory-to-understand-the-backlash-against-it/.

6. Cheryl I. Harris, "Whiteness as Property," *Harvard Law Review* 106, no. 8 (1993): 1707–91; Robin Bernstein, *Racial Innocence: Performing Childhood and Race from Slavery to Civil Rights* (New York: New York University Press, 2011).

7. Michael Warner, *Publics and Counterpublics* (New York: Zone Books, 2002).

8. Alex Abramovich and Jama Shelton, *Where Am I Going to Go? Intersectional Approaches to Ending LGBTQ2S Youth Homelessness in Canada & the U.S.* (Toronto: Canadian Observatory of Homelessness, 2017); Brandon Andrew Robinson, *Coming Out to the Streets: LGBTQ Youth Experiencing Homelessness* (Oakland: University of California Press, 2020); Cindy Cruz, "LGBTQ Street Youth Talk Back: A Meditation on Resistance and Witnessing," *International Journal of Qualitative Studies in Education* 24, no. 5 (2011): 547–58, https://doi.org/10.1080/09518398.2011.600270; Jen Reck, "Homeless Gay and Transgender Youth of Color in San Francisco: 'No One Likes Street Kids'—Even in the Castro," *Journal of LGBT Youth* 6, no. 2–3 (2009): 223–42, https://doi.org/10.1080/19361650903013519; Jama Shelton and Julie Winklestein, "Librarians and Social Workers: Working Together for Homeless LGBTQ Youth," *Young Adult Library Services* 13, no. 1 (2014): 20–24.

9. Kusenbach, "Street Phenomenology."

10. Justin Spinney, "Close Encounters? Mobile Methods, (Post)Phenomenology and Affect," *Cultural Geographies* 22, no. 2 (2015): 242, https://doi.org/10.1177/1474474014558988.

11. Mark Anthony Castrodale, "Mobilizing Dis/Ability Research: A Critical Discussion of Qualitative Go-along Interviews in Practice," *Qualitative Inquiry* 24, no. 1 (2018): 45–55, https://doi.org/10.1177/1077800417727765; Claire Edwards and Nicola Maxwell, "Troubling Ambulant Research: Disabled People's Socio-Spatial Encounters with Urban Un/Safety and the Politics of Mobile Methods," *Irish Journal of Sociology* 31, no. 1 (2022), https://doi.org/10.1177/07916035221098601.

12. Sam Stiegler, "Approaching Home: A Youth Worker Feeling Youth Work," in *Youth Sexualities: Public Feelings and Contemporary Cultural Politics* (vol. 2), ed. Susan Talburt (Santa Barbara, CA: Praeger, 2018), 3–12.

13. I received permission from the University of British Columbia's Behavioral Research Ethics Review Board to allow youth between the ages of fifteen and eighteen to consent for themselves if their parents were not supportive of the queerness or transness and asking for said permission would put them in danger. However, all the youth who participated were over eighteen years of age and could consent without parental permission.

14. Nicholas A. Scott, "Calibrating the Go-along for the Anthropocene," *International Journal of Social Research Methodology* 23 (2020): 2, https://doi.org/10.1080/13645579.2019.1696089.

15. Nancy Lesko and Susan Talburt, *Keywords in Youth Studies: Tracing Affects, Movements, Knowledges* (New York: Routledge, 2012).

16. Gloria Ladson-Billings, "Just What Is Critical Race Theory and What's It Doing in a Nice Field Like Education?" in *Race Is . . . Race Isn't: Critical Race Theory and Qualitative Studies in Education*, ed. Laurence Parker, Donna Deyhle, and Sofia Villenas (Boulder, CO: Westview Press, 1999), 7–30; Gloria Ladson-Billings and William F. Tate, "Toward a Critical Race Theory of Education," *Teachers College Record* 97, no. 1 (1997): 47–68.

17. Enke, "The Education of Little Cis."

18. There was an additional participant with whom I conducted one go-along, though I have chosen to exclude that participant and their go-along from this book. Elsewhere, I have discussed my initial reasoning for doing so, while reflecting on what this decision says about my own choices as a researcher. Sam Stiegler, "Walking to the Pier and Back," *Qualitative Inquiry* 28, no. 2 (2022): 200–208, https://doi.org/10.1177/10778004211042353.

19. Personal correspondence, September 25, 2016.

20. Castrodale, "Mobilizing Dis/Ability Research"; Scott, "Calibrating the Go-along for the Anthropocene"; Uwe Flick, Andreas Hirseland, and Benjamin Hans, "Walking and Talking Integration: Triangulation of Data from Interviews and Go-Alongs for Exploring Immigrant Welfare Recipients' Sense(s) of Belonging," *Qualitative Inquiry* 25, no. 8 (2019): 799–810, https://doi.org/10.1177/1077800418809515; Carolyn M. Porta et al., "Go-along Interviewing with LGBTQ Youth in Canada and the United States," *Journal of LGBT Youth* 14, no. 1 (2017): 1–15, https://doi.org/10.1080/19361653.2016.1256245; Sam Stiegler, "On Doing Go-along Interviews: Toward Sensuous Analyses of Everyday Experiences," *Qualitative Inquiry* 27, no. 3–4 (2021): 364–73, https://doi.org/10.1177/1077800420918891; Edwards and Maxwell, "Troubling Ambulant Research"; Richard M. Carpiano, "Come Take a Walk with Me: The 'Go-along' Interview as a Novel Method for Studying the Implications of Place for Health and Well-Being," *Health and Place* 15, no. 1 (2009): 263–72, https://doi.org/10.1016/j.healthplace.2008.05.003; Spinney, "Close Encounters?"

21. Phillip Vannini and April Vannini, "Wild Walking: A Twofold Critique of the Walk-along Method," in *Walking through Social Research*, ed. C. Bates and A. Rhys-Taylor (London: Routledge, 2017), 179.

22. Kathleen Stewart, *A Space on the Side of the Road: Cultural Poetics in an "Other" American* (Princeton, NJ: Princeton University Press, 1996), 2.

23. Ernesto Javier Martínez, *On Making Sense: Queer Race Narratives of Intelligibility* (Palo Alto, CA: Stanford University Press, 2012), 159.

24. Kathleen Stewart, "Worlding Writing," *Departures in Critical Qualitative Research* 5, no. 4 (2016): 96.

25. Petra Munro Hendry, "The Future of Narrative," *Qualitative Inquiry* 13, no. 4 (2007): 489, https://doi.org/10.1177/1077800406297673.

26. Elizabeth Ellsworth, *Places of Learning: Media, Architecture, Pedagogy* (New York: RoutledgeFalmer, 2005), 1.

27. José Esteban Muñoz, *Cruising Utopia: The Then and There of Queer Futurity* (New York: New York University Press, 2009), 189.

28. Eve Tuck and K. Wayne Yang, "Unbecoming Claims: Pedagogies of Refusal in Qualitative Research," *Qualitative Inquiry* 20, no. 6 (2014): 812, https://doi.org/10.1177/1077800414530265.

29. William F. Pinar, "The Unaddressed 'I' of Ideology Critique," *Power and Education* 1, no. 2 (2009): 189–200, https://doi.org/10.2304/power.2009.1.2.189; Judith Butler, "Giving an Account of Oneself," *Diacritics* 31, no. 4 (2001): 22–40, https://doi.org/10.1353/dia.2004.0002.

30. Tuck and Yang, "Unbecoming Claims," 811.

31. Irit Rogoff, "Looking Away: Participations in Visual Culture," in *After Criticism: New Responses to Art and Performance*, ed. Gavin Butt (Oxford: Blackwell, 2005), 119, https://doi.org/10.1002/9780470774243.ch6.

32. Ed Brockenbrough, "Introduction to the Special Issue: Queers of Color and Anti-Oppressive Knowledge Production," *Curriculum Inquiry* 43, no. 4 (September 23, 2013): 427, https://doi.org/10.1111/curi.12023.

Chapter 1

1. Christina B. Hanhardt, *Safe Space: Gay Neighborhood History and the Politics of Violence* (Durham, NC: Duke University Press, 2013); Jen Jack Gieseking, *A Queer New York: Geographies of Lesbians, Dykes, and Queers* (New York: New York University Press, 2020).

2. Maggie MacLure, "The Wonder of Data," *Cultural Studies ↔ Critical Methodologies* 13, no. 4 (May 8, 2013): 229, https://doi.org/10.1177/1532708613487863.

Chapter 2

1. As of March 2017, this library branch closed, as the site was slotted for a redevelopment project featuring a thirty-six-story mixed-use condominium tower, low-income housing units, a Department of Education computer lab, and a new, much larger, library branch for the Brooklyn Heights neighborhood. Mary Frost, "NYC Approves Demolition of Brooklyn Heights Library, Paving Way for Luxury Tower," *Brooklyn Daily Eagle*, March 6, 2017, http://www.brooklyneagle.com/articles/2017/3/6/nyc-approves-demolition-brooklyn-heights-library-paving-way-luxury-tower.

2. Cindy Cruz, "LGBTQ Street Youth Talk Back: A Meditation on Resistance and Witnessing," *International Journal of Qualitative Studies in Education* 24, no. 5 (2011): 556, https://doi.org/10.1080/09518398.2011.600270

Chapter 3

1. Toby Beauchamp, *Going Stealth: Transgender Politics and U.S. Surveillance Practices* (Durham, NC: Duke University Press, 2019).

2. Jian Neo Chen, *Trans Exploits: Trans of Color Cultures and Technologies in Movement* (Durham, NC: Duke University Press, 2018).

3. Janet Mock, *Redefining Realness: My Path to Womanhood, Identity, and So Much More* (New York: Artia, 2014).

4. Lisa Weems, "From 'Home' to 'Camp': Theorizing the Space of Safety," *Studies in Philosophy and Education* 29, no. 6 (September 2, 2010): 557–68, https://doi.org/10.1007/s11217-010-9199-2.

5. Margarethe Kusenbach, "Street Phenomenology: The Go-along as Ethnograhic Tool," *Ethnography* 4, no. 3 (2003): 455–85, https://doi.org/10.1177/146613810343007.

6. Mark Anthony Castrodale, "Mobilizing Dis/Ability Research: A Critical Discussion of Qualitative Go-along Interviews in Practice," *Qualitative Inquiry* 24, no. 1 (2018): 45–55, https://doi.org/10.1177/1077800417727765.

7. Issac West, *Transforming Citizenships: Transgender Articulations of the Law* (New York: New York University Press, 2014).

8. Cindy Cruz, "LGBTQ Street Youth Talk Back: A Meditation on Resistance and Witnessing," *International Journal of Qualitative Studies in Education* 24, no. 5 (2011): 557, https://doi.org/10.1080/09518398.2011.600270.

9. Reina Gossett, Eric A. Stanley, and Johanna Burton, *Trap Door: Trans Cultural Production and the Politics of Visibilty* (Cambridge, MA: MIT Press, 2017), xxiii.

Chapter 5

1. D. Wendy Greene, "Black Women Can't Have Blonde Hair . . . in the Workplace," *Journal of Gender, Race and Justice* 14, no. 2 (2011): 405–30.

2. Karolina Doughty and Lesley Murray, "Discourses of Mobility: Institutions, Everyday Lives and Embodiment," *Mobilities* 11, no. 2 (2016): 303–22, https://doi.org/10.1080/17450101.2014.941257.

3. Stephanie Pollack, Barry Bluestone, and Chase Billingham, "Maintaining Diversity in America's Transit-Rich Neighborhoods: Tools for Equitable Neighborhood Change" (Boston, MA: Dukakis Center for Urban and Regional Policy, 2010).

4. It is because of Anna's younger sister that Anna is in the study at all. She had not been to HMI for a long time before one day deciding to bring her fifteen-year-old sister in to become a member. On the day that she did so, I was working the front desk, and we were both excited to see each other. Explaining to her what I was doing back at HMI, she expressed interest in being part of the study.

5. Bettina L. Love, *Hip Hop's Li'l Sistas Speak: Negotiating Hip Hop Identities and Politics in the New South* (New York: Peter Lang, 2012); Dominique C. Hill, "Blackgirl, One Word: Necessary Transgressions in the Name of Imagining Black Girlhood," *Cultural Studies ↔ Critical Methodologies* 19, no. 4 (2019): 275–83, https://doi.org/10.1177/1532708616674994.

6. Ed Brockenbrough, "Queer of Color Agency in Educational Contexts: Analytic Frameworks from a Queer of Color Critique," *Educational Studies* 51, no. 1 (2015): 31, https://doi.org/10.1080/00131946.2014.979929.

7. Savannah Shange, *Progressive Dystopia: Abolition, Anti-Blackness, and Schooling in San Francisco* (Durham, NC: Duke University Press, 2019), 99–100.

Chapter 6

1. Toby Beauchamp, *Going Stealth: Transgender Politics and U.S. Surveillance Practices* (Durham, NC: Duke University Press, 2019).

2. Reina Gossett, Eric A. Stanley, and Johanna Burton, *Trap Door: Trans Cultural Production and the Politics of Visibilty* (Cambridge, MA: MIT Press, 2017).

3. Dean Spade, *Normal Life: Administrative Violence, Critical Trans Politics, and the Limits of the Law* (Brooklyn, NY: South End Press, 2011).

4. Aren Z. Aizura, "The Persistence of Transgender Travel Narratives," in *Transgender Migrations: The Bodies, Borders, and Politics of Transition*, ed. Trystan T. Cotten (New York: Routledge, 2012), 152.

5. Eric A. Stanley, "Near Life, Queer Death: Overkill and Ontological Capture," *Social Text* 29, no. 2 (2011): 3, https://doi.org/10.1215/0164247210.1215/01642472-1259461.

Chapter 7

1. A neighborhood in Brooklyn, DUMBO stands for Down Under the Manhattan Bridge Overpass.

2. Catherine Robinson, "Creating Space, Creating Self: Street-Frequenting Youth in the City and Suburbs," *Journal of Youth Studies* 3, no. 4 (2000): 429–43, https://doi.org/10.1080/713684388; Kelvin E. Y. Low, "The Sensuous City: Sensory Methodologies in Urban Ethnographic Research," *Ethnography* 16, no. 3 (2015): 295–312, https://doi.org/10.1177/1466138114552938.

3. Eve Tuck and Marcia McKenzie, "Relational Validity and the 'Where' of Inquiry: Place and Land in Qualitative Research," *Qualitative Inquiry* 21, no. 7 (2015): 3, https://doi.org/10.1177/1077800414563809.

4. T. Shildrick, "Youth Culture, Subculture and the Importance of Neighbourhood," *Young* 14, no. 1 (January 26, 2006): 61–74, https://doi.org/10.1177/1103308806059815.

5. Cindy Cruz, "LGBTQ Street Youth Talk Back: A Meditation on Resistance and Witnessing," *International Journal of Qualitative Studies in Education* 24, no. 5 (2011): 556. https://doi.org/10.1080/09518398.2011.600270.

6. Christina B. Hanhardt, *Safe Space: Gay Neighborhood History and the Politics of Violence* (Durham, NC: Duke University Press, 2013); Jen Jack Gieseking, *A Queer New York: Geographies of Lesbians, Dykes, and Queers* (New York: New York University Press, 2020).

7. Syed Ali, "I Gentrify Bed-Stuy," *Contexts* 13, no. 1 (2014): 84, https://doi.org/10.1177/1536504214522018.

8. Eve Tuck et al., "Geotheorizing Black/Land: Contestations and Contingent Collaborations," *Departures in Critical Qualitative Research* 3, no. 1 (2014): 52–74, https://doi.org/10.1525/dcqr.2014.3.1.52.

9. Jen Jack Gieseking, "Crossing over into Neighbourhoods of the Body: Urban Territories, Borders and Lesbian-Queer Bodies in New York City," *Area* 48, no. 3 (2016): 269, https://doi.org/10.1111/area.12147.

10. Zeus Leonardo, "The Souls of White Folk: Critical Pedagogy, Whiteness Studies, and Globalization Discourse," *Race Ethnicity and Education* 5, no. 1 (March 2002): 29–50, https://doi.org/10.1080/13613320120117180.

Chapter 8

1. Alecia Youngblood Jackson, "Posthumanist Data Analysis of Mangling Practices," *International Journal of Qualitative Studies in Education* 26, no. 6 (July 2013): 741–48, https://doi.org/10.1080/09518398.2013.788762.

2. Elizabeth Adams St.Pierre, "The Appearance of Data," *Cultural Studies ↔ Critical Methodologies* 13, no. 4 (May 8, 2013): 226, https://doi.org/10.1177/1532708613487862.

3. Maggie MacLure, "The Wonder of Data," *Cultural Studies ↔ Critical Methodologies* 13, no. 4 (May 8, 2013): 231, https://doi.org/10.1177/1532708613487863.

4. Susan Naomi Nordstrom, "Not So Innocent Anymore: Making Recording Devices Matter in Qualitative Interviews," *Qualitative Inquiry* 21, no. 4 (2015): 388–401, https://doi.org/10.1177/1077800414563804.

Chapter 9

1. Erica Rand, *The Small Book of Hip Checks: On Queer Gender, Race, and Writing* (Durham, NC: Duke University Press, 2021), 14.

2. Jack Halberstam, *The Queer Art of Failure* (Durham, NC: Duke University Press, 2011), 138.

3. Sarah de Leeuw, " 'If Anything Is to Be Done with the Indian, We Must Catch Him Very Young': Colonial Constructions of Aboriginal Children and the Geographies of Indian Residential Schooling in British Columbia, Canada,"

Children's Geographies 7, no. 2 (2009): 123–40; Robin Bernstein, *Racial Innocence: Performing Childhood and Race from Slavery to Civil Rights* (New York: New York University Press, 2011).

4. Steven Roberts, "Beyond 'NEET' and 'Tidy' Pathways: Considering the 'Missing Middle' of Youth Transition Studies," *Journal of Youth Studies* 14, no. 1 (2011): 21–39, https://doi.org/10.1080/13676261.2010.489604.

5. LJ Slovin, "What Grade Are You In? On Being a Non-Binary Researcher," *Curriculum Inquiry* 50, no. 3 (2020): 15, https://doi.org/10.1080/03626784.2020.1754730.

6. Gloria Anzaldúa, "To(o) Queer the Writer: Loca, Escritora, y Chicana," in *Living Chicana Theory*, ed. Carla Trujillo (Berkeley, CA: Third Woman Press, 1998), 263.

7. Finn Enke, "The Education of Little Cis: Cisgender and the Discipline of Opposing Bodies," in *Transfeminist Perspectives in and beyond Transgender and Gender Studies*, ed. Finn Enke (Philadelphia: Temple University Press, 2012); Slovin, "What Grade Are You In?"

8. Julia Sinclair-Palm, "'It's Non-Existent': Haunting in Trans Youth Narratives about Naming," *Occasional Paper Series* 37 (2017): 1–13.

9. Jen Gilbert, *Sexuality in Schools: The Limits of Education* (Minneapolis: University of Minnesota Press, 2014).

Chapter 10

1. Nancy Lesko, *Act Your Age: A Cultural Construction of Adolescence*, 2nd ed. (New York: Routledge, 2012); Mary Louise Adams, *The Trouble with Normal: Postwar Youth and the Making of Heterosexuality* (Toronto, ON: University of Toronto Press, 1997).

2. Sam Stiegler and Rachael E. Sullivan, "How to 'Fail' in School Without Really Trying: Queering Pathways to Success," *Pedagogy, Culture and Society* 23, no. 1 (2015): 65–83, https://doi.org/http://dx.doi.org/10.1080/14681366.2014.919956.

3. Angelina E. Castagno, *Educated in Whiteness: Good Intentions and Diversity in Schools* (Minneapolis: University of Minnesota Press, 2014).

4. Adam J. Greteman, "Lessons from the Leather Archives and Museum," *Journal of Curriculum Theorizing* 29, no. 2 (2013): 254–66.

5. Margarethe Kusenbach, "Street Phenomenology: The Go-along as Ethnographic Tool," *Ethnography* 4, no. 3 (2003): 455–85, https://doi.org/10.1177/146613810343007.

6. Tomas Boatwright, "Flux Zine: Black Queer Storytelling," *Equity & Excellence in Education* 52, no. 4 (2019): 383–95.

7. Sarah Pink, *Doing Visual Ethnography*, 2nd ed. (London: Sage, 2007), 62.

Chapter 11

1. Irit Rogoff, "Looking Away: Participations in Visual Culture," in *After Criticism: New Responses to Art and Performance*, ed. Gavin Butt (Oxford: Blackwell, 2005), 119.

2. Jon M. Wargo, " 'Every Selfie Tells a Story . . ': LGBTQ Youth Lifestreams and New Media Narratives as Connective Identity Texts," *New Media & Society* 19, no. 4 (2017): 560–78, https://doi.org/10.1177/1461444815612447.

Chapter 12

1. Jenna Burrell, "The Field Site as a Network: A Strategy for Locating Ethnographic Research," *Field Methods* 21, no. 2 (2009): 181–99, https://doi.org/10.1177/1525822X08329699.

2. Rob Shields, *The Virtual* (New York: Routledge, 2003).

3. Maria Lugones, "Playfulness, 'World'-Travelling, and Loving Perception," *Hypatia* 2, no. 2 (1987): 11, https://doi.org/10.1177/1461444815612447.

4. José Esteban Muñoz, *Cruising Utopia: The Then and There of Queer Futurity* (New York: New York University Press, 2009), 7.

Chapter 13

1. Danielle Brown, *East of Flatbush, North of Love* (New York: My People Tell Stories, LLC, 2016).

2. *BKReader*, "Black Homeownership Has Declined 13% in NYC over the Last Two Decades, New Report Finds," *BKReader*, March 18, 2021, https://www.bkreader.com/news/black-homeownership-has-declined-13-in-nyc-over-the-last-two-decades-new-report-finds-6546534.

Coda

1. Maggie MacLure, "Researching without Representation? Language and Materiality in Post-Qualitative Methodology," *International Journal of Qualitative Studies in Education* 26, no. 6 (July 2013): 660, https://doi.org/10.1080/09518398.2013.788755.

2. Elizabeth Freeman, *Time Binds: Queer Temporalities, Queer Histories* (Durham, NC: Duke University Press, 2010), xv.

3. Kathryn Bond Stockton, *The Queer Child, or Growing Sideways in the Twentieth Century* (Durham, NC: Duke University Press, 2009).

4. Michel de Certeau, *The Practice of Everyday Life* (Berkeley: University of California Press, 1984), 92.

5. Leigh Patel, *Decolonizing Educational Research: From Ownership to Answerability* (New York: Routledge, 2016).

6. Colson Whitehead, *The Colossus of New York* (New York: Anchor Books, 2003), 4.

7. Eve Tuck and Marcia McKenzie, *Place in Research: Theory, Methodology, and Method* (New York: Routledge, 2015).

8. Michel Foucault, *Discipline and Punish: The Birth of the Prison* (London: A. Lane, 1977); Lesko, *Act Your Age: A Cultural Construction of Adolescence*; Susan Talburt, "Constructions of LGBT Youth: Opening Up Subject Positions," *Theory into Practice* 43, no. 2 (2004): 116–21, https://doi.org/10.1207/s15430421tip4302_4; Sam Stiegler, " 'Getting to [Un]Know You': Opening Up Constructions and Imaginations of Youth," *Discourse* 38, no. 6 (2017): 892–905, https://doi.org/10.1080/01596306.2016.1187114.

9. Lance T. McCready, "A Double Life: Black Queer Youth Coming of Age in Divided Cities," *Educational Forum* 79, no. 4 (2015): 353–58, https://doi.org/10.1080/00131725.2015.1069516; Ed Brockenbrough and Tomas Boatwright, "In the MAC: Creating Safe Spaces for Transgender Youth of Color," in *Cultural Transformations: Youth and Pedagogies of Possibility*, ed. Korina Mineth Jocson (Cambridge: Harvard Education Press, 2013), 165–82; Jen Reck, "Homeless Gay and Transgender Youth of Color in San Francisco: 'No One Likes Street Kids'—Even in the Castro," *Journal of LGBT Youth* 6, no. 2–3 (2009): 223–42, https://doi.org/10.1080/19361650903013519; Lisa W. Loutzenheiser, "Working Alterity: The Impossibility of Ethical Research with Youth," *Educational Studies: Journal of the American Educational Studies Association* 41, no. 2 (2007): 109–27, https://doi.org/10.1080/00131940701312389.

10. Jeff Malpas, *Place and Experience* (Cambridge: Cambridge University Press, 1999).

11. Whitehead, *Colossus of New York*, 4–5.

12. de Certeau, *Practice of Everyday Life*, 93.

Bibliography

Abramovich, Alex, and Jama Shelton. *Where Am I Going to Go? Intersectional Approaches to Ending LGBTQ2S Youth Homelessness in Canada and the U.S.* Toronto, ON: Canadian Observatory of Homelessness, 2017.

Adams, Mary Louise. *The Trouble with Normal: Postwar Youth and the Making of Heterosexuality.* Toronto, ON: University of Toronto Press, 1997.

Aizura, Aren Z. "The Persistence of Transgender Travel Narratives." In *Transgender Migrations: The Bodies, Borders, and Politics of Transition*, edited by Trystan T. Cotten, 139–56. New York: Routledge, 2012.

Ali, Syed. "I Gentrify Bed-Stuy." *Contexts* 13, no. 1 (2014): 84. https://doi.org/10.1177/1536504214522018.

Anzaldúa, Gloria. "To(o) Queer the Writer: Loca, Escritora, y Chicana." In *Living Chicana Theory*, edited by Carla Trujillo, 263–76. Berkeley, CA: Third Woman Press, 1998.

Beauchamp, Toby. *Going Stealth: Transgender Politics and U.S. Surveillance Practices.* Durham, NC: Duke University Press, 2019.

Bernstein, Robin. *Racial Innocence: Performing Childhood and Race from Slavery to Civil Rights.* New York: New York University Press, 2011.

BKReader. "Black Homeownership Has Declined 13% in NYC over the Last Two Decades, New Report Finds." *BKReader*, March 18, 2021. https://www.bkreader.com/news/black-homeownership-has-declined-13-in-nyc-over-the-last-two-decades-new-report-finds-6546534.

Boatwright, Tomas. "Flux Zine: Black Queer Storytelling." *Equity & Excellence in Education* 52, no. 4 (2019): 383–95.

Brockenbrough, Ed. "Introduction to the Special Issue: Queers of Color and Anti-Oppressive Knowledge Production." *Curriculum Inquiry* 43, no. 4 (September 23, 2013): 426–40. https://doi.org/10.1111/curi.12023.

———. "Queer of Color Agency in Educational Contexts: Analytic Frameworks from a Queer of Color Critique." *Educational Studies* 51, no. 1 (2015): 28–44. https://doi.org/10.1080/00131946.2014.979929.

Brockenbrough, Ed, and Tomas Boatwright. "In the MAC: Creating Safe Spaces for Transgender Youth of Color." In *Cultural Transformations: Youth and Pedagogies of Possibility*, edited by Korina Mineth Jocson, 165–82. Cambridge, MA: Harvard Education Press, 2013.

Brown, Danielle. *East of Flatbush, North of Love*. New York: My People Tell Stories, LLC, 2016.

Burrell, Jenna. "The Field Site as a Network: A Strategy for Locating Ethnographic Research." *Field Methods* 21, no. 2 (2009): 181–99. https://doi.org/10.1177/1525822X08329699.

Butler, Judith. "Giving an Account of Oneself." *Diacritics* 31, no. 4 (2001): 22–40. https://doi.org/10.1353/dia.2004.0002.

Carpiano, Richard M. "Come Take a Walk with Me: The 'Go-along' Interview as a Novel Method for Studying the Implications of Place for Health and Well-Being." *Health and Place* 15, no. 1 (2009): 263–72. https://doi.org/10.1016/j.healthplace.2008.05.003.

Castagno, Angelina E. *Educated in Whiteness: Good Intentions and Diversity in Schools*. Minneapolis: University of Minnesota Press, 2014.

Castrodale, Mark Anthony. "Mobilizing Dis/Ability Research: A Critical Discussion of Qualitative Go-along Interviews in Practice." *Qualitative Inquiry* 24, no. 1 (2018): 45–55. https://doi.org/10.1177/1077800417727765.

Certeau, Michel de. *The Practice of Everyday Life*. Berkeley: University of California Press, 1984.

Chen, Jian Neo. *Trans Exploits: Trans of Color Cultures and Technologies in Movement*. Durham, NC: Duke University Press, 2018.

Cruz, Cindy. "LGBTQ Street Youth Talk Back: A Meditation on Resistance and Witnessing." *International Journal of Qualitative Studies in Education* 24, no. 5 (2011): 547–58. https://doi.org/10.1080/09518398.2011.600270.

Doughty, Karolina, and Lesley Murray. "Discourses of Mobility: Institutions, Everyday Lives and Embodiment." *Mobilities* 11, no. 2 (2016): 303–22. https://doi.org/10.1080/17450101.2014.941257.

Edwards, Claire, and Nicola Maxwell. "Troubling Ambulant Research: Disabled People's Socio-Spatial Encounters with Urban Un/Safety and the Politics of Mobile Methods." *Irish Journal of Sociology* 31, no. 1 (2022). https://doi.org/10.1177/07916035221098601.

Ellsworth, Elizabeth. *Places of Learning: Media, Architecture, Pedagogy*. New York: RoutledgeFalmer, 2005.

Enke, Finn. "The Education of Little Cis: Cisgender and the Discipline of Opposing Bodies." In *Transfeminist Perspectives in and beyond Transgender and Gender Studies*, edited by Finn Enke, 60–77. Philadelphia: Temple University Press, 2012.

Flick, Uwe, Andreas Hirseland, and Benjamin Hans. "Walking and Talking Integration: Triangulation of Data from Interviews and Go-Alongs for Exploring

Immigrant Welfare Recipients' Sense(s) of Belonging." *Qualitative Inquiry* 25, no. 8 (2019): 799–810. https://doi.org/10.1177/1077800418809515.

Foucault, Michel. *Discipline and Punish: The Birth of the Prison*. London: A. Lane, 1977.

Freeman, Elizabeth. *Time Binds: Queer Temporalities, Queer Histories*. Durham, NC: Duke University Press, 2010.

Frost, Mary. "NYC Approves Demolition of Brooklyn Heights Library, Paving Way for Luxury Tower." *Brooklyn Daily Eagle*, 2017. http://www. brooklyneagle.com/articles/2017/3/6/nyc-approves-demolition-brooklyn-heights-library-paving-way-luxury-tower.

Gieseking, Jen Jack. *A Queer New York: Geographies of Lesbians, Dykes, and Queers*. New York: New York University Press, 2020.

———. "Crossing over into Neighbourhoods of the Body: Urban Territories, Borders and Lesbian-Queer Bodies in New York City." *Area* 48, no. 3 (2016): 262–70. https://doi.org/10.1111/area.12147.

Gilbert, Jen. *Sexuality in Schools: The Limits of Education*. Minneapolis: University of Minnesota Press, 2014.

Gill-Peterson, Jules. "From Gender Critical to QAnon: Anti-Trans Politics and the Laundering of Conspiracy." *New Inquiry*, September 13, 2021.

Gossett, Reina, Eric A. Stanley, and Johanna Burton. *Trap Door: Trans Cultural Production and the Politics of Visibility*. Cambridge, MA: MIT Press, 2017.

Greene, D. Wendy. "Black Women Can't Have Blonde Hair . . . in the Workplace." *Journal of Gender, Race and Justice* 14, no. 2 (2011): 405–30.

Greteman, Adam J. "Lessons from the Leather Archives and Museum." *Journal of Curriculum Theorizing* 29, no. 2 (2013): 254–66.

Halberstam, Jack. *The Queer Art of Failure*. Durham, NC: Duke University Press, 2011.

Hanhardt, Christina B. *Safe Space: Gay Neighborhood History and the Politics of Violence*. Durham, NC: Duke University Press, 2013.

Harris, Cheryl I. "Whiteness as Property." *Harvard Law Review* 106, no. 8 (1993): 1707–91.

Hendry, Petra Munro. "The Future of Narrative." *Qualitative Inquiry* 13, no. 4 (2007): 487–98. https://doi.org/10.1177/1077800406297673.

Hill, Dominique C. "Blackgirl, One Word: Necessary Transgressions in the Name of Imagining Black Girlhood." *Cultural Studies ↔ Critical Methodologies* 19, no. 4 (2019): 275–83. https://doi.org/10.1177/1532708616674994.

Jackson, Alecia Youngblood. "Posthumanist Data Analysis of Mangling Practices." *International Journal of Qualitative Studies in Education* 26, no. 6 (July 2013): 741–48. https://doi.org/10.1080/09518398.2013.788762.

Kusenbach, Margarethe. "Street Phenomenology: The Go-along as Ethnographic Tool." *Ethnography* 4, no. 3 (2003): 455–85. https://doi.org/10.1177/146613810343007.

Ladson-Billings, Gloria. "Just What Is Critical Race Theory and What's It Doing in a Nice Field Like Education?" In *Race Is . . . Race Isn't: Critical Race Theory and Qualitative Studies in Education*, edited by Laurence Parker, Donna Deyhle, and Sofia Villenas, 7–30. Boulder, CO: Westview Press, 1999.

Ladson-Billings, Gloria, and William F. Tate. "Toward a Critical Race Theory of Education." *Teachers College Record* 97, no. 1 (1997): 47–68.

Leeuw, Sarah de. "'If Anything Is to Be Done with the Indian, We Must Catch Him Very Young': Colonial Constructions of Aboriginal Children and the Geographies of Indian Residential Schooling in British Columbia, Canada." *Children's Geographies* 7, no. 2 (2009): 123–40.

Leonardo, Zeus. "The Souls of White Folk: Critical Pedagogy, Whiteness Studies, and Globalization Discourse." *Race Ethnicity and Education* 5, no. 1 (March 2002): 29–50. https://doi.org/10.1080/13613320120117180.

Lesko, Nancy. *Act Your Age: A Cultural Construction of Adolescence*. 2nd ed. New York: Routledge, 2012.

Lesko, Nancy, and Susan Talburt. *Keywords in Youth Studies: Tracing Affects, Movements, Knowledges*. New York: Routledge, 2012.

Loutzenheiser, Lisa W. "Working Alterity: The Impossibility of Ethical Research with Youth." *Educational Studies: Journal of the American Educational Studies Association* 41, no. 2 (2007): 109–27. https://doi.org/10.1080/00131940701312389.

Love, Bettina L. *Hip Hop's Li'l Sistas Speak: Negotiating Hip Hop Identities and Politics in the New South*. New York: Peter Lang, 2012.

Low, Kelvin E. Y. "The Sensuous City: Sensory Methodologies in Urban Ethnographic Research." *Ethnography* 16, no. 3 (2015): 295–312. https://doi.org/10.1177/1466138114552938.

Lugones, Maria. "Playfulness, 'World'-Travelling, and Loving Perception." *Hypatia* 2, no. 2 (1987): 3–19. https://doi.org/10.1177/1461444815612447.

MacLure, Maggie. "Researching without Representation? Language and Materiality in Post-Qualitative Methodology." *International Journal of Qualitative Studies in Education* 26, no. 6 (July 2013): 658–67. https://doi.org/10.1080/09518398.2013.788755.

———. "The Wonder of Data." *Cultural Studies ↔ Critical Methodologies* 13, no. 4 (May 8, 2013): 228–32. https://doi.org/10.1177/1532708613487863.

Malpas, Jeff. *Place and Experience*. Cambridge: Cambridge University Press, 1999.

Martínez, Ernesto Javier. *On Making Sense: Queer Race Narratives of Intelligibility*. Palo Alto, CA: Stanford University Press, 2012.

McCready, Lance T. "A Double Life: Black Queer Youth Coming of Age in Divided Cities." *The Educational Forum* 79, no. 4 (2015): 353–58. https://doi.org/10.1080/00131725.2015.1069516.

Mock, Janet. *Redefining Realness: My Path to Womanhood, Identity, and So Much More*. New York: Artia, 2014.

Muñoz, José Esteban. *Cruising Utopia: The Then and There of Queer Futurity*. New York: New York University Press, 2009.

Nordstrom, Susan Naomi. "Not So Innocent Anymore: Making Recording Devices Matter in Qualitative Interviews." *Qualitative Inquiry* 21, no. 4 (2015): 388–401. https://doi.org/10.1177/1077800414563804.

Patel, Leigh. *Decolonizing Educational Research: From Ownership to Answerability*. New York: Routledge, 2016.

Pinar, William F. "The Unaddressed 'I' of Ideology Critique." *Power and Education* 1, no. 2 (2009): 189–200. https://doi.org/10.2304/power.2009.1.2.189.

Pink, Sarah. *Doing Visual Ethnography*. 2nd ed. London: Sage, 2007.

Pollack, Stephanie, Barry Bluestone, and Chase Billingham. "Maintaining Diversity in America's Transit-Rich Neighborhoods: Tools for Equitable Neighborhood Change." Boston: Dukakis Center for Urban and Regional Policy, 2010.

Porta, Carolyn M., Heather L. Corliss, Jennifer M. Wolowic, Abigail Z. Johnson, Katie Fritz Fogel, Amy L. Gower, Elizabeth M. Saewyc, and Marla E. Eisenberg. "Go-along Interviewing with LGBTQ Youth in Canada and the United States." *Journal of LGBT Youth* 14, no. 1 (2017): 1–15. https://doi.org/10.1080/19361653.2016.1256245.

Rand, Erica. *The Small Book of Hip Checks: On Queer Gender, Race, and Writing*. Durham, NC: Duke University Press, 2021.

Reck, Jen. "Homeless Gay and Transgender Youth of Color in San Francisco: 'No One Likes Street Kids'—Even in the Castro." *Journal of LGBT Youth* 6, no. 2–3 (2009): 223–42. https://doi.org/10.1080/19361650903013519.

Roberts, Steven. "Beyond 'NEET' and 'Tidy' Pathways: Considering the 'Missing Middle' of Youth Transition Studies." *Journal of Youth Studies* 14, no. 1 (2011): 21–39. https://doi.org/10.1080/13676261.2010.489604.

Robinson, Brandon Andrew. *Coming out to the Streets: LGBTQ Youth Experiencing Homelessness*. Oakland: University of California Press, 2020.

Robinson, Catherine. "Creating Space, Creating Self: Street-Frequenting Youth in the City and Suburbs." *Journal of Youth Studies* 3, no. 4 (2000): 429–43. https://doi.org/10.1080/713684388.

Rofes, Eric. "Bound and Gagged: Sexual Silences, Gender Conformity and the Gay Male Teacher." *Sexualities* 3, no. 4 (2000): 439–62. https://doi.org/10.1177/136346000003004005.

Rogoff, Irit. "Looking Away: Participations in Visual Culture." In *After Criticism: New Responses to Art and Performance*, edited by Gavin Butt, 117–34. Oxford: Blackwell, 2005. https://doi.org/10.1002/9780470774243.ch6.

Scott, Nicholas A. "Calibrating the Go-along for the Anthropocene." *International Journal of Social Research Methodology* 23 (2020): 317–28. https://doi.org/1 0.1080/13645579.2019.1696089.

Shange, Savannah. *Progressive Dystopia: Abolition, Anti-Blackness, and Schooling in San Francisco*. Durham, NC: Duke University Press, 2019.

Shelton, Jama, and Julie Winklestein. "Librarians and Social Workers: Working Together for Homeless LGBTQ Youth." *Young Adult Library Services* 13, no. 1 (2014): 20–24.

Shields, Rob. *The Virtual*. New York: Routledge, 2003.

Shildrick, T. "Youth Culture, Subculture and the Importance of Neighbourhood." *Young* 14, no. 1 (January 26, 2006): 61–74. https://doi.org/10.1177/1103308806059815.

Silin, Jonathan G. "Teaching as a Gay Man: Pedagogical Resistance or Public Spectacle?" *GLQ: A Journal of Lesbian and Gay Studies* 5, no. 1 (1999): 95–106.

Sinclair-Palm, Julia. " 'It's Non-Existent': Haunting in Trans Youth Narratives about Naming." *Occasional Paper Series* 37 (2017): 1–13.

Slovin, LJ. "What Grade Are You In? On Being a Non-Binary Researcher." *Curriculum Inquiry* 50, no. 3 (2020): 1–17. https://doi.org/10.1080/03626784.2020.1754730.

Spade, Dean. *Normal Life: Administrative Violence, Critical Trans Politics, and the Limits of the Law*. Brooklyn, NY: South End Press, 2011.

Spinney, Justin. "Close Encounters? Mobile Methods, (Post)Phenomenology and Affect." *Cultural Geographies* 22, no. 2 (2015): 231–46. https://doi.org/10.1177/1474474014558988.

St. Pierre, Elizabeth Adams. "The Appearance of Data." *Cultural Studies ↔ Critical Methodologies* 13, no. 4 (May 8, 2013): 223–27. https://doi.org/10.1177/1532708613487862.

Stanley, Eric A. "Near Life, Queer Death: Overkill and Ontological Capture." *Social Text* 29, no. 2 (2011): 1–19. https://doi.org/10.1215/0164247210.1215/01642472-1259461.

Stewart, Kathleen. *A Space on the Side of the Road: Cultural Poetics in an "Other" American*. Princeton, NJ: Princeton University Press, 1996.

———. "Worlding Writing." *Departures in Critical Qualitative Research* 5, no. 4 (2016): 95–99.

Stiegler, Sam. "Approaching Home: A Youth Worker Feeling Youth Work." In *Youth Sexualities: Public Feelings and Contemporary Cultural Politics* (vol. 2), edited by Susan Talburt, 3–12. Santa Barbara, CA: Praeger, 2018.

———. " 'Getting to [Un]Know You': Opening Up Constructions and Imaginations of Youth." *Discourse* 38, no. 6 (2017): 892–905. https://doi.org/10.1080/01596306.2016.1187114.

———. "On Doing Go-along Interviews: Toward Sensuous Analyses of Everyday Experiences." *Qualitative Inquiry* 27, no. 3–4 (2021): 364–73. https://doi.org/10.1177/1077800420918891.

———. "Walking to the Pier and Back." *Qualitative Inquiry* 28, no. 2 (2022): 200–208. https://doi.org/10.1177/10778004211042353.

Stiegler, Sam, and Rachael E Sullivan. "How to 'Fail' in School without Really Trying: Queering Pathways to Success." *Pedagogy, Culture and Society* 23,

no. 1 (2015): 65–83. https://doi.org/http://dx.doi.org/10.1080/14681366.20
14.919956.

Stockton, Kathryn Bond. *The Queer Child, or Growing Sideways in the Twentieth Century*. Durham, NC: Duke University Press, 2009.

Stovall, David, and Subini Annamma. "Using Critical Race Theory to Understand the Backlash to It." *The Hechinger Report*, July 29, 2021. https://hechingerreport.org/opinion-using-critical-race-theory-to-understand-the-backlash-against-it/.

Talburt, Susan. "Constructions of LGBT Youth: Opening Up Subject Positions." *Theory into Practice* 43, no. 2 (2004): 116–21. https://doi.org/10.1207/s15430421tip4302_4.

Tuck, Eve, and Marcia McKenzie. *Place in Research: Theory, Methodology, and Method*. New York: Routledge, 2015.

———. "Relational Validity and the 'Where' of Inquiry: Place and Land in Qualitative Research." *Qualitative Inquiry* 21, no. 7 (2015): 1–6. https://doi.org/10.1177/1077800414563809.

Tuck, Eve, Mistinguette Smith, Allison M. Guess, Tavia Benjamin, and Brian K. Jones. "Geotheorizing Black/Land: Contestations and Contingent Collaborations." *Departures in Critical Qualitative Research* 3, no. 1 (2014): 52–74. https://doi.org/10.1525/dcqr.2014.3.1.52.52.

Tuck, Eve, and K. Wayne Yang. "Unbecoming Claims: Pedagogies of Refusal in Qualitative Research." *Qualitative Inquiry* 20, no. 6 (2014): 811–18. https://doi.org/10.1177/1077800414530265.

Vannini, Phillip, and April Vannini. "Wild Walking: A Twofold Critique of the Walk-along Method." In *Walking through Social Research*, edited by C. Bates and A. Rhys-Taylor, 179–95. London: Routledge, 2017.

Wargo, Jon M. " 'Every Selfie Tells a Story . . .': LGBTQ Youth Lifestreams and New Media Narratives as Connective Identity Texts." *New Media & Society* 19, no. 4 (2017): 560–78. https://doi.org/10.1177/1461444815612447.

Warner, Michael. *Publics and Counterpublics*. New York: Zone Books, 2002.

Weems, Lisa. "From 'Home' to 'Camp': Theorizing the Space of Safety." *Studies in Philosophy and Education* 29, no. 6 (September 2, 2010): 557–68. https://doi.org/10.1007/s11217-010-9199-2.

West, Issac. *Transforming Citizenships: Transgender Articulations of the Law*. New York: New York University Press, 2014.

Whitehead, Colson. *The Colossus of New York*. New York: Anchor Books, 2003.

Index

ability, 3–4, 15, 36, 39–40, 43–44, 48–51, 61–63, 80–81, 83, 91, 104, 138. *See also* disability; safety
academic support, 13
access, accessibility, 5, 8–9, 13, 15, 36–38, 82, 103–4, 117–18, 139–40; to bathrooms, 48–50; home and, 46–47, 50–51
adulthood, 16, 63, 95–99
adult stores, 64–68
affect, 12–13, 20–21. *See also* individual affects by name
age, 3–4, 12–14, 16, 141–42, 144n13. *See also* youth
agency, 50, 64
AmeriCorps, 96–97
anxiety, 72–73, 111–12, 117
Anzaldúa, Gloria, 98
art, 124; arts and culture programs, 13

ballroom, 13
"bathroom bills," 48
BDSM, 102–3
beauty, 60. *See also* clothing; hair
Beyoncé, 41, 72
binder, chest, 97–98
Black, 15, 35, 38, 40, 106; Black girls (#BlackGirlMagic, Black girl ordinary), 64; Black women, 60,

63–64; neighborhoods in NYC, 1–2, 8–9, 17–18, 83–85, 101, 104, 125–26. *See also* race
blame, 73–74
body: dancing and, 61–63; gender and, 72–73, 75–78, 93–95, 97–100; housing and, 83; identity and, 99–100; interpreting, 40–41; normative standards of, 60; reading, 16–18, 98–99; in relation to others, 69–70, 104; in research, 25–27, 32–33, 40–41, 54, 57–58, 104, 132–33; time and, 47; youth and, 63, 140–41
Brockenbrough, Ed, 28–29, 64
Brooklyn Public Library, 35–40
Burton, Johanna, 50

cash assistance benefits, 44–45
catcalling, 33
Christianity, 5–6. *See also* religion
cisgender, cisness, 1–2, 16–17, 25–26, 44, 77, 98, 102, 143n2
City University of New York (CUNY), 15, 102
class, 8–9; norms of, 140–41; public transit and, 61; race and, 125–26; sexuality and, 97–98
clothing, 93–94, 96–98, 100. *See also* shopping

colonialism, 95–96, 140; settler colonialism, 25–28

commuting, 9–10, 19, 59–60, 64, 79–80, 82, 107

companionship, 112–13, 117–18. *See also* relationality

confusion, 63, 72–74, 77, 85–86, 113–14

consent, 2–4, 10–11, 19, 39, 70–71, 102–5, 112, 114, 116–17, 127–28, 144n13

critical race theory, 5–6, 16–17

cruising, 95

Cruz, Cindy, 50, 83

dancing, 61–63, 66–67

data, 6–7, 19–21, 23, 137–38; engagement with, 33–34; lost, 89–92. *See also* research

dating, 62–63, 95–96, 115–16

de Certeau, Michel, 140, 142

decision-making, 11–12

demisexuality, 115–16

desire, 5–6, 20–21, 33–34, 36, 48, 94–95, 114–15; gender and, 50, 71–74, 98–99, 115–16; race and, 60, 62–63

disability, 8, 12, 140–42. *See also* ability

discipline, 73–74, 76, 99–100, 140–42

displacement, 37, 40. *See also* housing

dysphoria, 71–72, 75

economics, 8–9, 83, 125–26. *See also* class

education, 2–3, 5, 8–9, 28–30, 103; spaces outside of, 10–11

Ellsworth, Elizabeth, 24–25

Enke, Finn, 16–17, 143n2

everyday, everydayness, 1–5, 10–13, 20–21; crossing borders and, 85; experiences that matter, 63–64;

housing insecurity and, 45–46; identity and, 15; norms of, 8; obstacles, 44; queer of color, 64; in research, 103–6

fatigue, 77

feminism of color, 16–17, 44

field site. *See under* research

food, 8–9, 11–12, 18, 105

freedom, 49, 102; financial, 62–63; mobile, 13–14, 124. *See also* agency

Freeman, Elizabeth, 139–40

gender, gender identity, 8–9; access to facilities and, 98–99; affirming, 71–73; body and, 93–95, 97–100; clothing and, 93–94, 97–98; disciplining of, 99–100; fatigue and, 77; femininity and, 71–73, 76, 93–94, 98–99; as incomplete, 98; knowledge and, 63–64; legibility of, 70–71, 74–75; masculinity and, 8–9, 76, 94–95, 99, 104; misgendering, 48, 69–70; movement and, 99–100; names and, 71–72; norms of, 63, 73–78, 97–100, 102, 140–41; passing, 73; policing, 70–71, 74–77, 137; pop culture and, 72; presentation, 43–44, 46–47; privilege and, 47; proving, 44–45; public spaces and, 15; race and, 8–9, 106; reading, 12–13, 16–17, 25–26, 48, 69–70, 72–73; representation and, 98–99; scrutiny of, 70, 104; safety and, 48; sexuality and, 90; surveillance of, 139–40; transitioning and, 112; youth and, 5–6, 16, 99–100

genderfluid, 1–2, 101, 126–28

genderqueer, 33, 70–71, 74–75, 98–99

gentrification, 32–33, 83–84, 126

Gieseking, Jen Jack, 85

girls, girlhood, 64. *See also* Black girl ordinary
go-along, 1–4, 6–8, 10–14; analyzing, 19–21, 54–56; as methodology, 21–25, 103–6, 137–38; individual experience and, 20–21; mobility and, 47; positionality and, 15–19; recording, 89–92. *See also* research
Gossett, Reina, 50
Grindr, 111, 113–16
group shelters, 36–38, 109–10, 113. *See also* housing
gym, 53–58, 94–95, 98–99

hair, 60
Halberstam, Jack, 95–96
harassment, 48
health care, 5, 8–9, 13
Hendry, Petra, 24
Hetrick-Martin Institute (HMI), 3, 8–10, 13–14, 19, 37–39, 127–18, 131–33
hip check, 93–94
HIV, 110, 139–40
hooking up, 114–16
hope, 121–22
housing, 8–9, 46–47; body and, 83; displacement and, 37, 40; homelessness, 10–12, 15; insecurity, 15, 43–44; knowledge of city and, 83; LGBTQ youth and, 109–10, 113; norms of, 114; property ownership and, 125–26; social media and, 114–15; space and, 15, 36, 40; support services, 13, 43–46; time and, 48–50

identity, 15; body and, 99–100; city and, 138–40; critical approaches to, 16–19; demographics and, 50–51; desire and, 115–16; knowledge and, 40–41, 83–85; as personal, 38–41; place and, 140–42; proving, 43–44, 46–47; racial, 86; scrutiny of, 70
immigration, 125–26
Indigenous peoples, 84
interruption, 132
intersectionality, 63, 83
intimacy, 11–13, 19, 31–32, 35, 56, 102, 115, 123

Judaism, 71–72, 75, 85–86
job training, 13, 110

kinship. *See* companionship
knowledge: of city, 80–87, 135–36, 138–42; as contingent, 140–42; disciplinary, 140–41; experience and, 83–85, 103; gender and, 63–64; identity and, 16–17, 40–41; making, 6–8; movement and, 11–14, 21–22, 37–38, 40, 54–55; narrative and, 22–25; norms of, 27–29; as philosophy, 63–64; of place, 106–7; queer of color, 28–29; race and, 63–64; savviness and, 39–40, 114–15; self-created, 63–64; settler colonialism and, 25–28; sharing, 87; of social services, 44–45, 48–49; spatialized, 80–86; subjectivity and, 23; unlearning, unknowing, 27; youth and, 63–64, 81, 114–15, 138–42
Kusenbach, Margarethe, 20–21

Ladson-Billings, Gloria, 16–17
Latinx, 8–9, 15, 50–51, 53–54, 121–22, 125–26
legibility, 43–44, 74–75
lesbian, 97–98
library, 35–40, 48
Lugones, Maria, 121–22

MacLure, Maggie, 33–34, 91

marijuana, 111–12
Martínez, Ernesto Javier, 23
McKenzie, Marcia, 81
mental health, 13
Metronome (public art installation), 43
Metropolitan Transit Authority (MTA), 61, 81–82. *See also* public transportation
Middle Eastern, 71–72, 75
Minaj, Nicki, 67
Mock, Janet, 44
mourning, 50–51
movement, mobility, 11–14, 18–19, 31–33; appearance and, 43–44; freedom of, 13–14; gender and, 70–71, 75–77, 99–100; identity and, 15; immobility and inaction, 45–47; knowledge and, 21–22, 37–38, 40, 54–55; of others, 36; positionality and, 83–85; public transportation and, 61–63, 76–82, 85–87; risk and, 70–71; solitary, 18–19; stillness and, 39–41, 51, 137; through urban space, 20–21, 31–33, 45–46, 54–55, 61–63, 70–71, 76–87, 106–7, 114–15, 136–42; through virtual worlds, 121–22; urgency of, 39–40; visibility and, 50
Muñoz, José Esteban, 24–25, 121–22

name, naming, 71–72, 98–99, 140–41
narrative, narrativization, 7–8, 19–25
nation, nationality, 14, 140–42
neutrality, 6–8
New York City, 138–39; becoming and, 81; Bedford-Stuyvesant (Bed-Stuy), 83–85; Bensonhurst, 9–10; Bronx, 59–60; Brooklyn, 35–36; Central Park, 89, 92; Christopher Street Pier, 8–9, 32–33; Coney Island, 79–81; East Flatbush, 32,

101–7, 125–27; Eastchester, 64; Greenwich Village, 13; Harlem, 32; Javits Center, 81–82; LaGuardia Airport, 135–36; Lincoln Center, 109–12, 117–18; Manhattan, 32; Metropolitan Museum of Art, 116–17; Midtown, 47; moving through, 11–14, 20–21, 31–33; neighborhoods, 1–2, 8–12, 17–18, 83–85, 101, 104, 125–26; Parkchester, 9–10; place and, 14; Ridgewood, 9–10; Rockefeller Center, 119–23; Staten Island Ferry, 46–47; Union Square, 43, 49–51, 93; Upper West Side, 32; West Village, 8–9
non-binary. *See* trans, queer, and non-binary (TQNB)
norms, normativity: adulthood and, 98; city and, 81; constraints of, 1–6, 81; everyday and, 8; gender and, 43–44, 63, 73–78, 97–100; homelessness and, 114; living amidst, 73–74; nonconformity, 70, 77–78; pathologizing queer, trans, and racialized students, 102; race and, 43–44, 63, 98, 102, 121–22; research and, 6–8, 19; sexuality and, 43–44, 116, 121–22; youth and, 114, 140–42

oppression, 73–74, 84–85

participant, 15–19, 23–24, 28–30, 127–29. *See also* positionality; researcher
perception, perspective, 2, 6, 12–13, 15–16, 20–23, 25–26, 48, 54–55, 64–65, 69–72, 74, 76, 101, 115–16, 135–42
philosophy, 63–64
photography, 110–12, 114–15

Pink, Sarah, 106–7
place, 9–10, 14; as contextually
  constituted, 81, 83–85; home
  and, 46–47; identity and, 140–42;
  knowledge of, 106–7; movement
  and, 20–21. *See also* space
police, policing, 8–9, 47, 70–71,
  74–77, 137, 139–40. *See also*
  surveillance
positionality, 4–5, 13–17; critical
  approaches to, 16–19; of
  participant, 15–19, 24, 28–30,
  83, 127–29; of reader, 27–28; of
  researcher, 16–19, 24–30, 54–58, 76,
  127–29, 131–33; youth and, 137–42
potential, 22–24, 28, 50, 96–97, 103,
  121–22, 142
power, 27, 63, 73–74, 84–85, 136–37,
  140–41
privacy, 38–39, 46–47
privilege, 4–5, 8–9, 16–17, 140;
  movement and, 15–16; racial,
  83–84, 86; of researcher, 25–27, 47,
  54–56, 76, 104; of time and space,
  50–51
property, 5–6, 125–26
proximity, 19, 28–29, 40–41, 69–70,
  95
public. *See under* space
public transportation, 8–10, 59–64,
  68, 76–82, 85–87
Pulse Nightclub, 50–51

queer, queerness. *See* trans, queer, and
  non-binary (TQNB)
queer and trans theory, 14, 16–17,
  24–25

race, 8–9; class and, 125–26; desire
  and, 62–63; ethnicity and, 53–54,
  71, 86, 91–92; gender and, 106;
  identity and, 86, 106; knowledge
and, 63–64; neighborhoods, 1–2,
  8–12, 17–18, 83–85, 101, 104,
  125–26; norms of, 3–4, 63, 98, 102,
  121–22, 140–41; privilege and, 47,
  83–84, 86; property and, 5–6, 125–
  26; public spaces and, 15; public
  transportation and, 61; queerness
  and, 2; reading, 12–13, 16–18,
  25–26; respectability and, 95–96;
  sexuality and, 38, 97–98; signifiers
  of, 71; surveillance of, 139–40;
  trans and queer communities and,
  83–84; whiteness and, 5–6, 16–18,
  47, 76, 83–84, 86, 98, 102, 104, 126;
  youth and, 16, 138–39
Rand, Erica, 93–94
recording devices, 89–92
reflection, 61–63
relationality: companionship and,
  112–13, 117–18; to others, 36,
  69–70, 103; reciprocal, 56–58;
  of research, 25–29; researcher-
  participant, 66, 70–71, 76,
  94–95, 101, 103–6, 127–29,
  131–32; student-teacher, 59–60;
  transactional, 105; virtual, 121–22
relaxation, 39–41
religion, 15–16, 71–72, 75, 83, 85–86;
  attacks on TQNB youth, 5–6
representation, 98–99, 114
research, 6–8, 19–24; as analytical
  target, 23–30, 54–56, 91–92,
  127–29, 131–33; body and, 32–33,
  40–41, 54, 57–58, 104, 132–33;
  boundaries, 6–8; closure and,
  31–34, 133; colonial gaze and, 140;
  data and, 91–92, 137–38; ethics
  of, 24; field sites, 121–22; looking
  away and, 28; methodology, 22–25,
  136–37; norms of, 19–21, 27–29;
  participation in, 38–39, 54–56; as
  process, 27–28, 33–34; settler

research (continued)
 colonial knowledge and, 25–27;
 wholeness and, 142. See also data;
 go-along
researcher, 16–19, 23–30, 54–58,
 76, 127–29, 131–33. See also
 positionality
respectability, 43–44, 95–96
restrooms, 48. See also access,
 accessibility
risk, 19, 37, 70–73
Rogoff, Irit, 28, 114

safety, 19, 43–44, 48
sanctuary, 36
savviness, 39–40, 60, 114–15
Scott, Nicholas A., 15
sensation. See perception, perspective
sex toys, 64–65
sexuality: class and, 97–98; gender
 and, 90; norms of, 3–4, 102, 116,
 121–22, 140–41; race and, 38,
 97–98; youth and, 5–6
shame, 73–74
Shange, Savannah, 64
shopping, 93–94, 96–98, 100, 119–23
Slovin, LJ, 96
Smith, Dee, 38
sobriety, 44–45
social media, 110–16
social service agencies, 44–45, 48–49
space, 9–10; being present in, 13;
 knowledge of, 80–87; mobility and,
 13–16; online, 114–16, 121–22;
 ownership of, 36, 45–46; personal,
 69–70; privilege of, 50–51; public,
 12–13, 15, 106–7, 114–16, 139–42;
 research and, 11–13; restrictions
 on, 47; strategic use of, 37–38, 40;
 taking up, 39–41, 69–71; urban,
 20–21

Spinney, Justin, 12
St. Pierre, Elizabeth, 91
Stanley, Eric A., 50, 77–78
Stewart, Kathleen, 22–24
subjectivity, 23, 77–78, 83. See also
 positionality
subway. See public transportation
success, 6–7, 44, 48–49, 68, 95–96, 98
surveillance, 47, 50, 70–71, 76–77,
 83, 104, 139–40. See also police,
 policing
survival, 37, 114, 139–40

time, temporality: future and, 49–50,
 61–62, 74, 95–96, 98, 121–22,
 139–40, 142; housing insecurity
 and, 46–50; as investment, 59–60;
 long stretches of, 61–62, 64;
 privilege of, 50–51; queer senses
 of, 24–25; speed of, 139–40; youth
 and, 139–40
trans, queer, and non-binary (TQNB):
 cisness and, 98, 102, 143n2;
 gendered power systems and, 48,
 73–78, 90, 99–100; job training,
 110; knowledge about, 6–8, 28–29;
 living and being, 77–78; mobile
 freedom of, 13–14, 31–33; parents
 and guardians, 13–14; public
 scrutiny of, 1–6; race and, 43–44,
 48, 83–84; transitioning and, 74–75,
 112; virtual worlds and, 121–22;
 visibility and, 50, 70–72, 75–78;
 youth and, 1–5, 10–13
Trans Day of Action, 110
transparency, 6–8
trust, 28–29, 60, 67–68, 103
Tuck, Eve, 25–26, 81

Vannini, Phillip and April, 20–21
victim, victimizing, 73–74, 117

video games, 119–24
violence, 50–51, 142
visibility, 50; of researcher, 54–56; trans, 70–72, 75–78

walk-along. *See* go-along
white supremacy, 5–6. *See also* whiteness *under* race
Whitehead, Colson, 140–42
wonder, 91
world-making, 6–8
writing: as process, 6–8, 27–28, 33–34; style of, 20–25

Yang, K. Wayne, 25–26

youth, 5–6, 16; adulthood and, 95–97; at-risk, 37; body and, 63, 140–41; as category, 142; gender and, 99–100; "good kid," 102; home and, 15, 46–47, 114; knowledge and, 63–64, 81–85, 114–15, 138–42; mobility practices of, 13–14, 18–19; normativity and, 3–4, 140–42, positionality of, 137–42; race and, 138–39; reading, 12–13; time and, 139–40; visual images and, 114–15. *See also* adulthood
youth centers, 3, 45–46, 109–10, 113, 128
YouTube, 35, 38, 40–41